"The ability to speak in front of a group is a very important tool. *Taking the Stage* teaches you that your opinions are as valuable as anyone else's. I have certainly seen members of my team more willing to speak up after participating in the 'Taking the Stage' program."

—**Richard Nesbitt, CEO, world markets, and COO, CIBC**

"The 'Taking the Stage' program has profoundly impacted IBM women at all levels, encouraging them to speak up, communicate for impact, and become essential to their clients."

—**Lauren O'Donnell, global general manager and vice president,
life sciences industry, IBM**

"It is with excitement that I endorse Judith Humphrey's book. She is an excellent communicator and I wish her every success in delivering her powerful and helpful messages to a wide audience. *Taking the Stage* will touch thousands of women around the world in the most positive ways."

—**Micheline Bouchard, former CEO, Motorola Canada,
and board member, International Women's Forum**

"Over the past 10 years, our firm has been reporting on the unacceptably low numbers of women in senior executive positions. Those figures will change dramatically—for the better!—when women read Judith Humphrey's compelling new book, *Taking the Stage*. I will certainly be recommending it to all my female clients, and to those who have women on their teams."

—**Jay Rosenzweig, CEO, Rosenzweig & Company**

"I love *Taking the Stage*. It spoke to me profoundly as I read it while on the subway in Seoul. It showed that we can embrace both the yin and yang, the female and male aspects of our natures. I truly believe that when we are able to harness both, we become better, stronger leaders. Judith Humphrey's brilliant book will show readers how to do just that."

—**Sharon Tan, vice president, HR/OD,
Asia, Grohe Pacific PTE LTD**

TAKING THE STAGE

HOW WOMEN CAN SPEAK UP, STAND OUT, AND SUCCEED

Judith Humphrey

JB JOSSEY-BASS™
A Wiley Brand

Published by Jossey-Bass
A Wiley Brand
One Montgomery Street, Suite 1200, San Francisco, CA 94104–4594—www.josseybass.com

Jossey-Bass books and products are available through most bookstores. To contact Jossey-Bass directly call our Customer Care Department within the U.S. at 800–956–7739, outside the U.S. at 317–572–3986, or fax 317–572–4002.

Wiley publishes in a variety of print and electronic formats and by print-on-demand. Some material included with standard print versions of this book may not be included in e-books or in print-on-demand. If this book refers to media such as a CD or DVD that is not included in the version you purchased, you may download this material at http://booksupport.wiley.com. For more information about Wiley products, visit www.wiley.com.

Taking the Stage® is a registered trademark of The Humphrey Group Inc., used by John Wiley & Sons under license for this publication.

The Leader's Script®, Speaking as a Leader®, Leadership Conversations®, Leadership Presence™, and Succeeding on Stage™ are trademarks of The Humphrey Group Inc.

Library of Congress Cataloging-in-Publication Data
Humphrey, Judith, 1943-
  Taking the stage: how women can speak up, stand out, and succeed/Judith Humphrey.
   1 online resource.
  Includes index.
  Description based on print version record and CIP data provided by publisher; resource not viewed.
  ISBN 978-1-118-95840-7 (pdf) — ISBN 978-1-118-95839-1 (epub) — ISBN 978-1-118-87025-9 (hardback)
  1. Women executives. 2. Leadership in women. 3. Communication in management. 4. Public speaking for women. 5. Oral communication. 6. Career development. I. Title.
  HD6054.3
  658.4'09082—dc23

                                                                              2014023068

Printed in the United States of America

FIRST EDITION

HB Printing   10 9 8 7 6 5 4 3 2

For Marc, my wonderful husband, who has always believed in me.
For Bart and Ben, who have shown that a woman can have bright,
happy, and cherished children and a successful career.

Contents

Preface

This book grows out of my conviction that confident self-expression is the foundation of success in business and life. I have seen the lives of thousands of women transformed when they learned to "take the stage." Graduates of our firm's Taking the Stage® program have found—as readers of this book will discover—how to *speak up, stand out, and succeed* in ways that increase their visibility, earn them respect, and accelerate their advancement. Many inspiring stories of those who have achieved these goals fill the pages of this book. I'm pleased to share with readers the insights from our program, from my twenty-five years as head of a communications company, and from my own life.

How do you know if this book is for you? If you would like a stronger voice in discussions; if you wish to express yourself with more clarity and impact; if you want others not to interrupt you because they don't "hear" you; if you'd like to be assertive but not aggressive, promote yourself, be visible, speak with presence, and move your career forward by showing yourself as a confident, capable leader—if you say "yes" to any of these, then this book is for you. *Taking the Stage* is a metaphor for all the ways you can be your own best champion by finding compelling ways to express yourself. Whatever your rank, position, or industry, this book is for all women who want to claim their right to confident self-expression and respect from others in the boardroom—and beyond. The rewards are enormous. So, take the stage!

This is a book for *women*, but it is also for *those who support women's success*. It is for leaders of women who want to build stronger, more diverse teams, or who have wives, female partners, or daughters they would like to see succeed. Men have told me, "I want a copy of this book for my wife, who can project more confidence," and "This would be useful for my daughter who is very smart but doesn't interview well." More broadly, this work is for anyone who cares about women, the future of young women, and the value that women can add to every business, profession, community, and family— when they do speak up and stand out as strong, confident leaders.

The message of this book is that women must take the stage if they want to have a greater impact on their organizations and greater success in their careers and lives. That journey into the spotlight requires a "center-stage mindset" and the ability to communicate in an inspiring, effective way. Success for women also requires support from their bosses, mentors, and sponsors. Executives and senior managers who lead women will find at the end of each chapter "Advice for Leaders of Women" that will enable them to support and coach the women in their lives and reinforce the teachings in this work.

Taking the Stage provides readers with a *proven, practical* approach developed by The Humphrey Group in our work with women. My own experience coaching and training was the starting point in my thinking that women must be stronger communicators if they want to succeed— at work and in life. I encouraged each woman I coached to be bolder, stronger, and more confident in her communications—skills that this book teaches. Today our firm has thirty-five instructors and coaches who work with both men and women to make them more confident, inspiring communicators and leaders. Our business is global, and our results are impressive. The ideas, techniques, and successes described in this text reflect our work with clients.

The book also embodies the experience of the many women who have attended our Taking the Stage program—or facilitated it—in locations around the world. I have come to know some of these women personally. Many others have generously shared their growth and courage with me in phone interviews, conference calls, and emails. The women whose stories appear in this book come from all geographies, all industries, and all levels of their organizations. In most cases, I've changed their names and personal details to protect their privacy. But the words and experiences they contributed are accurately reflected in the quoted passages. I am grateful to these brave women—this book could never have been written without their inspiring stories. Taking the Stage is based on original research—our "lab" being The Humphrey Group's work with women and our feedback from firms where more than four hundred thousand women have graduated from our Taking the Stage program. This has given us a powerful source of insight that has shaped our assumptions about how women communicate in business and beyond.

Taking the Stage also complements an impressive recent body of literature that emphasizes the communications challenges women face and their need to speak up more boldly and successfully. These works include Sheryl Sandberg's *Lean In*, Barbara Annis and John Gray's *Work with Me*, and Katty Kay and Claire Shipman's *The Confidence Code*. These works continue the debate about whether women's communication style is a reflection of "nature" or "nurture." But even with this diversity of viewpoints there is consensus that women *can take action* to build their own confidence and strengthen their voices in ways that will have a positive and sustained impact on their lives. *Taking the Stage* focuses on the ACTIONS women can take to develop stronger, more powerful voices and achieve confident communications leadership in all situations—whether they are making a presentation, chatting at a networking event, or pitching an idea.

This book emerges from my own personal journey as well. *Taking the Stage* is a metaphor for my life. Growing up in a small town in Connecticut, I dreamed of the vast world "out there" and was determined to find a bigger "stage" on which to express myself. The courage that I developed allowed me to move from one field to another: from music, to university teaching, to the corporate world, and finally to my own company. Each stage was larger and filled with more opportunity—though it was never easy transitioning from one stage to the next. And now, looking back, I see that all the qualities I discuss in this book—such as assertiveness, confidence, and a willingness to speak up—were necessary and gradually became part of my self-definition. So this book reflects hard-earned passages in my own life.

Finally, this book deals with qualities and desires deep within all of us. It is our birthright to be heard. We were born with voices—loud, penetrating voices—and there is absolutely no reason why women should feel obliged to surrender those voices in the face of obstacles. This book is ultimately an affirmation of our life force.

TAKING THE STAGE

Introduction

I n January 2001, I sat down to prepare a speech that I would deliver to 350 women managers and executives. Though I had enthusiastically accepted this opportunity to promote my firm, I felt a pang of regret after agreeing to speak.

The prospect was daunting. Although I had spoken to smaller groups of forty or fifty people, I had never addressed such a large business audience. I wouldn't be able to "chat" with them as I did with more intimate gatherings; I might not even be able to see them, with the stage lights in my eyes. To add to the pressure, my company—The Humphrey Group—had spent the past decade teaching *others* how to speak. Many of the women in my audience were executives who recently had received speech coaching from us—or from *me personally*. They'd likely expect flawless execution from me as head of the firm. Despite the fact that I'd prepared and rehearsed several times, I took the podium with some trepidation.

No wonder my opening words were: "Talk about pressure!" I added that now "the shoe—or the high heel—was on the other foot," because *I* was the one being scrutinized. That moment of honesty grounded me and made them laugh. I went on to tell the women in the room that "this is what it means to take the stage." I continued, "Every time you walk up to that podium, or stand in front of an audience, or meet with a client or a boss, there are expectations that you'll influence and inspire your listeners." I then introduced my main message: "While we women all too often are reluctant to take the stage, we can and *must* do so if we want to realize our capacity for leadership."[1]

1

The speech was an awakening for me—a realization that I *did* have it in me to take the stage in front of such a large group. The speech was transformational for my audience because so many in the room had never heard this message before. The concept of "taking the stage" had come to me as a result of all the coaching I and my colleagues had provided to women. Initially, we had trained mostly men—C-suite executives who wanted to be superb speakers. Gradually, as more and more women entered the picture, it became obvious that—unlike many of the men we'd trained—women were uncomfortable in the spotlight. We realized that they needed special encouragement to overcome their sense of inadequacy, put themselves out there, and speak as strong, confident leaders.

This was the first time I had delivered that message, and there was stillness in the room as I spoke. I had never seen such rapt attention. Afterward, the attendees approached me and urged me to create a seminar that would show them and the women reporting to them how to take the stage. We now offer that seminar both publicly and in-house to our client companies.

I am grateful to the women who were in that room that day and for the tens of thousands of women around the world who have attended our Taking the Stage program since then. They have taught me about the deep desire so many women have to express themselves more fully and more confidently. They have shown me the power of this book's message: women must come out from the wings and take the stage if they want to have a greater impact on their organizations and their own careers.

Overview of the Book

I've written this book so women can find their own strong voices, seize new opportunities to lead, and advance their careers. If women lack confidence, as Katty Kay and Claire Shipman make clear in their superb book, *The Confidence Code*, then it's time for women to take action on their own behalf.[2] *Taking the Stage* puts forth a compelling strategy for reversing traditional female socialization, thereby helping us become more comfortable in the spotlight. It will show you how to take your rightful place on the corporate stage to advance yourself and your ideas. The Humphrey Group's work with tens of thousands of women for more than twenty-five years has given us a powerful source of insight that has shaped our assumptions about how women communicate in business and beyond.

The book has four parts.

Part 1 discusses how you can "Choose to Take the Stage." Here you will learn how to take the stage *mentally*. It all begins with the conscious choice to come out from the wings and be fearless in your desire to be heard, every day—even when others may not agree with you. It means finding the confidence to accept that others want to see, hear, and be led by you. You'll discover how to silence that inner voice that says "You shouldn't speak up now," or "You can't add any value to this discussion." You will learn how to feel comfortable speaking up, discussing your accomplishments, showing courage, and holding your ground when others seek to undercut you or dissuade you from taking the stage.

Part 2 shows readers how to "Create a Strong Script"—either one that's written or one that's simply in your mind. Here you will discover how to take the stage *verbally*. Every time we speak—whether at the podium, at meetings, in one-on-one encounters, or on the phone—we create scripts. Sometimes we only have time to create a brief mental outline of what we want to say; in other instances we can put pen to paper. Whatever the format, your script should portray you and your ideas in the best light. Unfortunately, many women undermine their leadership by crafting weak scripts that call attention to their perceived inadequacies, or present them as perpetually busy, always sorry, often worried, confused, or stressed. A woman might say, "I'm sorry, it was my fault," "Don't mind me, I'm having a bad day," "I'm buried in work." This part of the book will show you how to script yourself as a confident leader, not only with strong language, but also with a clear message, a persuasive structure, an opening grabber that gets the audience's attention, and a closing call to action. You will learn how to craft compelling scripts for all situations—from formal meetings and career discussions to elevator conversations.

Part 3 explains how to "Unlock the Power of Your Voice." Here you will discover how to take the stage *vocally*. We should use our voices as instruments of leadership; yet many women reduce this power by softening or sweetening their tones, or rushing so no one can interrupt them. They also often lift their voices at the end of sentences, which makes them sound as though they are asking a question rather than speaking decisively. Such "upspeak" makes women sound unsure of themselves. This part will teach you to overcome such minimizing vocal patterns and reclaim the true power of your voice.

Part 4 shows you how to "Stand Out on Stage." Here you will learn how to take the stage *physically*. Having a strong physical presence is important for leaders and shows others that you are confident and capable. Women often project a less than confident physical presence. Their minimizing body language can involve everything from poor posture, small gestures, and furtive or weak eye contact to ingratiating facial expressions and clothing that distracts from their leadership. This part of the book shows you how to project a strong, self-affirming physical presence.

In sum, the four parts of the book will make clear how to take the stage *mentally*, *verbally*, *vocally*, and *physically*.

This book does not advocate that women try to become men or simply agree to play by men's rules. Rather, *Taking the Stage* calls on women to develop a more forceful approach to leadership and to make certain that their voices and ideas are heard. Self-confidence and assertiveness do not belong to men alone, although these qualities are often associated with the "male" style of leadership. Such strengths are a woman's birthright, too.

Nor does arguing that women need to become bolder and more assertive suggest that we should dismiss the special qualities women bring to their leadership. Dr. Judy Rosener writes in a *Harvard Business Review* article, "Ways Women Lead," that "effective leaders don't come from one mold . . . [Women's] nontraditional leadership style is well suited to the conditions of some work environments and can increase an organization's chances of surviving in an uncertain world."[3] Indeed, women's collaborative style of leadership is critical to today's organizations. Women listen well, demonstrate empathy, work well together, and can be extremely supportive. Women are also more likely to develop other women.[4] In their book *The Athena Doctrine*, John Gerzema and Michael D'Antonio aptly conclude that "the world would be a better place if men thought more like women."[5]

But by themselves, the "female" qualities of leadership can produce an overemphasis on *others* and an underemphasis on *ourselves*. With such a focus, many women lose out on jobs, promotions, kudos, air time, and power. Women need to supplement their "female" approach with the self-assertiveness that men display. If women follow the path recommended in this book, they will be embracing both what we think of as "male" and "female" qualities and achieving a holistic leadership style.

How difficult will it be for women to develop this new style of leadership, which combines "male" and "female" qualities? And to put the issue more broadly, how difficult will it be for corporate cultures to change? Some assert that there are "social norms that are so gendered and so stereotyped that even though we think we've gone past them, we really haven't."[6] But in the firms that want to make progress in this area, much has been accomplished. Changing the course of history—or corporate history—is not easy. It's time now for women to move beyond negative assumptions and look to themselves for the courage and determination needed to rise through the ranks and create a new model for female leadership.

Male leaders also have a vested interest in this positive transformation of female leadership. John Montalbano, chief executive officer of RBC Global Asset Management, told me in an interview, "If you have a strong culture, the professionals in your organization have a keen interest in winning. Winning ultimately means having the best talent around the table. And when you identify great talent regardless of gender or race, you must foster it and allow it to have a meaningful contribution within the organization."

Our Time Is Now!

Why is the need for this book so pressing? In some respects women have made great strides. Women today are more educated and professionally ready than they have ever been. Young women are now more likely than young men to enroll in and graduate from higher education.[7] Women receive nearly 60 percent of college degrees, up from one-third in 1960.[8] Some have called this the "feminization of higher education."[9]

But despite those gains in education and the increasing number of women in professional programs, study after study shows that very few females reach the higher echelons of leadership and power. Women's progress up the corporate ladder—in America and around the world—by all accounts has been painfully slow.[10] The *New York Times* sums it up: "Men still control the most important industries, especially technology, occupy most of the positions on the lists of the richest Americans, and continue to make more money than women who have similar skills and education."[11]

This lack of progress hurts companies as well as individual women. Studies by the research firm Catalyst show that corporations in which more women are on the board and in the top executive ranks have higher earnings and better returns on investment.[12] Women are not only important consumers, their values shape our society in ways that differ from their male counterparts. They are also an extraordinary source of talent. Companies ignore them at great risk to the bottom line.

In a *Fortune* magazine article, Warren Buffet emphasizes his belief that promoting women makes for good business. He writes, "Women are a major reason we will do so well . . . We've seen what can be accomplished when we use 50% of our human capacity. If you visualize what 100% can do, you'll join me as an unbridled optimist about America's future." He concludes, "Fellow males, get on board."[13]

The implications of Taking the Stage extend far beyond personal development. We in The Humphrey Group have seen a huge groundswell in corporate commitment to this program. It's no longer just women who see this need. Male executives champion this program because they want their organizations to perform at the highest possible levels. One male head of an investment banking division was the first in his organization to introduce our program to two hundred women and, coupled with other initiatives and development programs, the results have been remarkable. His talent pool has grown and women are increasingly being promoted into the executive ranks. More women at the firm are making it clear to their managers that they believe their performance warrants consideration for a promotion. As part of the selection process, the women used all their Taking the Stage skills to impress the committee and get promoted into the executive suite. So the future lies in our own hands.

How Women Will Advance

Steps by corporations, governments, and other groups are key in helping women advance. Still, the philosophy that underlies this book is that women *themselves* must accelerate their upward climb. *They need to show others they are confident, capable leaders who believe in themselves and can inspire that belief in others.* They must act on their own behalf by taking the stage.

Taking the stage involves speaking up, being forthright, expressing your viewpoint in meetings. It means not pulling back when challenged or when your inner voice seeks to undermine you. It means accepting praise for a job well done, rather than saying, "It was nothing" or "My team did it." It means stepping up to whatever opportunity presents itself, and having the strength to say, "Here's what I believe." It also means putting yourself forward for leadership roles or more senior positions, even though you may feel you're not fully qualified. In large and small ways, it involves showing the world (and yourself) that you are a person to be reckoned with and that you believe in yourself and can inspire others to believe in you too. This path involves risk, but the rewards of having your voice heard and being respected for speaking up far outweigh the uncertainties you may feel as you step forward.

This process of taking the stage is indeed the most important thing women can do for themselves if they want to advance. The stage provides a positive, motivational metaphor for women who wish to succeed in the business world. The "glass ceiling" suggests a limitation on what women can achieve—that they will eventually bang their heads against a hidden barrier that will keep them from reaching their companies' top echelons. In contrast, the stage is a rich and positive metaphor for women's advancement. Every day provides women with new opportunities to shine on some sort of stage—in boardrooms, meeting rooms, offices, conference and lecture halls, and in chance encounters in corridors and elevators.

As founder and past president of a global consulting firm, I have seen that women's communication style comprises their greatest challenge. This is true regardless of rank, culture, or industry. Too often women are reluctant to speak up in meetings; to apply for new positions; to pose new ideas or challenge someone else who has spoken. They are hesitant to discuss their accomplishments. They undersell themselves in job interviews and business interactions. They minimize themselves mentally, verbally, vocally, and physically when they speak. Their style is weaker and less compelling than is needed for them to lead others. The result is that many women sideline themselves, rather than standing in the spotlight and telling others confidently what they think.

On a daily basis we receive feedback and written testimonials making clear that the program that has inspired this book helps women succeed. One manager observed, "Your program has changed my life. The impact at first was subtle: I stopped nodding my head, as though agreeing with everything everybody said. I also stopped apologizing and I began to stand up straighter. I started dressing differently—more professionally. I volunteered to lead safety meetings in our Hydro office. I am more focused on where I am going because I now set career goals whereas before I had never really set goals. People perceive me as more of a leader."

Another woman told us, "I'm in a male-dominated industry and petite. What I've learned is that I have to be able to stand up to men that are three times my size and say, 'Look, I'm serious. I know what I'm talking about and this is how it's going to be.' 'Yes, Ma'am' is their response when I talk that way."

Taking the stage doesn't always involve major, career-changing events; it might simply mean raising one's hand in a meeting, offering to lead a project, providing a dissenting opinion. The starting point is to realize that you are *always on stage*—whether you are in your firm's cafeteria or at a networking event with senior executives, customers, or peers.

This learning applies in your personal and community life as well as the business world. One woman explained, "I'm a member of the board of governors of a private golf club, along with twelve men. I had always sat quietly and let the men discuss the finances and other topics; I was reluctant to say, 'Well, hang on a minute; *this* is what we need to do.' Since completing Taking the Stage I have definitely spoken up and the men have paid attention. I have gotten a lot of positive comments and was recently elected to be the president of our association!"

Such opportunities make up the life of any business woman. The success you have in these situations will depend on your ability to recognize these as leadership moments, and to know how to seize these opportunities to influence and inspire. Now, more than ever, it's time for women to take the stage. This book will give you a new way of looking at yourself, a new center-stage mind-set and skills, and a stronger resolve to move beyond whatever external barriers you face and seize every opportunity to shine and succeed in your career and in life.

Part One

Choose to Take the Stage

Chapter One

We Have Been Taught to Fit In, Not Stand Out

G rowing up, I didn't fit in. I had four sisters who were always together—ice skating, sledding, playing with our animals, dating cute guys, and going to camp, where they met still more friends. But I did not feel part of this youthful euphoria. I remember lying awake at night, counting the days in an average life span, just to get some measure of how long I'd have to endure this isolation. We lived in a very small town where no buses, trains, or taxis stopped. I often wished I could run down to the end of our road and signal a bus to stop and take me anywhere else.

My way out was the violin, which transported me from this social and rural isolation to a glorious world where I could be alone yet connected to something larger than myself—a world of music, of the Masters, of teachers who believed in me, and universities that welcomed my musical talent. Though my parents made it clear they did not want me to become a musician—too Bohemian a lifestyle—I chose my own path and financially fended for myself. Through part-time work, loans, and a fellowship, I managed to support myself and get two master's degrees.

This sense of autonomy pushed me to go further. I bought a Triumph motorcycle in grad school and taught a community course on "Feminism."

My college boyfriends called me a "modern woman." I became increasingly comfortable taking the stage as the years went by—and I enjoyed more success in doing so.

Most women are socialized to fit in—to seek self-definition through acceptance by others. And many women who acted in accordance with the expectations of others probably had an easier time growing up than I did. But if they want to get ahead in business they must confront a hard reality: their socialization has made them less comfortable than men are standing out and claiming their place in the spotlight. Only when women understand these formative influences can they move beyond their socialization and embody the mindset of a leader.

Girls Are Taught to Fit In

Let's begin with our earliest social interactions on the playground. In her book *Talking from 9 to 5: Women and Men at Work*, author Deborah Tannen explains, "Boys are expected to put themselves forward, emphasize the qualities that make them look good, and deemphasize those that would show them in a less favorable light. . . . Girls are expected to be 'humble'—not try to take the spotlight, emphasize the ways they are just like everyone else, and deemphasize ways they are special. A woman who does this really well comes off as lacking in confidence."[1]

Starting in childhood, girls learn that sounding too sure of themselves will make them unpopular with their peers. A group of girls might ostracize a schoolmate who shows too much pride in her accomplishments by saying, "Look at her, she's got attitude" or "Who does she think she is?" A girl who tells others what to do is called "bossy." As girls we learned that it is bad to stand out or be too successful. I experienced this when I received a fellowship to pursue my graduate program in English literature. I called home with the good news, and my dad admonished me, "Don't get too many degrees. The boys won't like you." It didn't stop me from moving forward with my education, but I wondered at the time if he might be right.

My female clients often speak about their own socialization in these terms. One female executive told me, "I spend a lot of time trying to build others up. I was often being tapped for leadership situations in high school, and always was embarrassed about it. I felt if I was doing achievement-oriented things in school or in my social life I'd try to soften them so people wouldn't turn against me. I kept saying, 'It's no big deal.' And I see myself doing that same kind of minimizing now."

Another woman, Terry, remembers her childhood with sadness: "I was a quiet, shy child. But I can recall one instance when I was organizing a game with my friends, and found myself getting excited in this youthful leadership role. I was almost shouting to one friend, 'Let's do this,' and to another, 'You stand there.' I felt really great. Then my mother heard this and reprimanded me for speaking too boldly. 'Terry, be quieter,' she said. After that, I kept my voice down."

Girls learn to express themselves in ways that sound neither too aggressive nor too certain. I was one of five girls, and I still remember my mother saying firmly more than a few times, "No arguing! No bickering! I didn't have five daughters so they could fight—I had them so they could be best friends." Girls raised with these norms adopt a collegial sharing of power that rewards uniformity and ensures that one person does not achieve a status higher than any others.

Doreen Lorenzo, president of product development company Quirky, echoes this perspective: "Girls are taught to be cooperative more than boys. I don't think girls get the tools they need in school to get that self-assuredness. In high school, girls want to be part of the tribe, so they're not stepping out of line. The boys are often the jocks, with much more bravado."[2] This inclusiveness hurts women when the time comes for them to stand out, whereas boys develop a social dynamic based on being one up or one down the ladder as they compete for the top position.

Even girls who were tomboys as youngsters seem eventually to fall into line. One female client told me, "There is a constant 'push' and 'pull' going on in my mind when I use 'me/mine' language. I'm afraid of being bold, arrogant, and aggressive. As a child, I didn't hold back. I was involved in lots of schoolyard fights. But I settled down when I got to high school. As I've grown older, the gender identity thing came into play. I don't like that I was aggressive as a child and have tried to compensate for that as an adult."

Women Are Reluctant to Stand Out

These childhood habits stay with us into adulthood. As women, we're uncomfortable in the boardroom or any other business situation when all eyes are on us. Expressing a dissenting idea can be nerve-wracking.

Women managers and executives often feel most comfortable in guiding or nurturing roles, where they can focus on *others* instead of themselves. They are at ease, for example, talking to their teams, because status is conferred in that situation. They provide valuable direction and receive positive feedback. Women also find comfort in being the organization's "worker bees," because they don't have to stand out; they can feel like behind-the-scenes contributors.

But when they have to sell their ideas and earn others' respect, women's socialization holds them back. Patsy Rodenburg, British voice coach and author of the essay "*Powerspeak:* Women and Their Voices in the Workplace," writes that whereas "male communication habits revolve around taking up space. Not giving in . . . Female habits revolve around reduction, denial, giving way, and not taking up space."[3] As Rodenburg explains, these tendencies toward "reduction" extend to our choice of words, the way we frame our thoughts, the way we express our voices—even the way we stand or sit in a chair. Such self-effacing behavior can characterize not only junior women but often the most senior women as well.

Many of the female senior executives I coach are almost embarrassed to be "in the spotlight" and undercut themselves when "too much" attention is lavished on them. One CEO I observed before she began her coaching stood in front of her audience, at an angle to them, cocked her head as if asking permission to speak, swayed back and forth, and spoke in a soft and halting voice—even though she was speaking about her company's extraordinary growth. She confessed that she felt like an imposter when she was center stage.

This kind of discomfort in the spotlight is something women at all levels experience. It can take the form of nervousness in front of a large audience, reluctance to express one's voice in a meeting, hesitation to apply for a career opportunity, or preference for observing others rather than speaking. We in The Humphrey Group have seen countless examples of women's reluctance to come forward into the spotlight. Here are just a few:

- A C-suite executive told me: "When I am asked to comment in a meeting on my work or speak about an issue at a management meeting, I don't know what to say. When I speak, I feel constantly rushed, my eyes fly everywhere, and I look as though I lack self-confidence. People must wonder how I ever made it to senior vice president."
- A manager in a global logistics firm said, "I often have stage fright and don't like to get up in front of a group of people—so I just do a *speed* presentation; I rush through it as fast as I can. I am more comfortable working with people who are within my area."
- A senior banker told me that "when there is a restructuring, the men go to the new head of the group and say 'I'd love to work for you.' The women wait until someone comes to them." And that rarely happens.
- When a bank president visited a team of eight HR women, they politely listened, but when he opened the floor to dialogue *not one* of the women spoke. As a result, they missed an opportunity to gain visibility.
- A female engineer said, "I love to observe and see what other people are doing. I'm not really interested in getting my opinion heard."
- A young newly hired woman was delighted to be attending a client meeting with her "mentor"; however, she stayed silent throughout because her mentor did not introduce her into the conversation.

Not all women are reluctant to stand out. But many we work with say they avoid being the center of attention. This is a systemic issue for women. They find clever and counterproductive ways either to avoid the spotlight or to minimize themselves and their power when they do become the focus of attention. Some may not be aware of what they're doing; but if they continue to retreat to the wings, they risk diminishing themselves—and paying a high price for it.

These behaviors reflect patterns of communicating in which women seek to AVOID sounding too strong, too successful, too sure of themselves. They adopt strategies for fitting in, not standing out. Scenarios like these are played out on the corporate stage every day; they suggest why women as a group are not progressing. Women in general don't have a *center-stage* mentality. They prefer to stand aside and make *others* look good.

If We Don't Stand Out, We Can't Be Outstanding

We have been taught to "fit in" and now must learn to "stand out." We must get rid of these minimizing behaviors and become comfortable being the ones others truly listen to. You can't get ahead in business—or anywhere else, for that matter—unless you can influence others; and you can't do that unless you are the one they're listening to.

To achieve this goal we must reverse the impact of our socialization by taking the stage, selling ourselves in every situation—delivering strong, clear, and compelling messages about ourselves and our ideas. This means showing a willingness to "go for it" and not backing down when the going gets tough.

Taking the stage is a metaphor for the transformation necessary for women if they want to succeed at higher levels. Those on stage get heard— and get promoted. Every chapter in this book will empower you to achieve the goal of successfully standing out.

And in *standing out*, you will have the opportunity to be seen as *outstanding*.

Advice for Leaders of Women

Women's preference for being "in the wings" is often the result of socially conditioned behavior. It does not reflect their true ability or desire to contribute. You can develop your female talent—and strengthen your team—by encouraging women to stand out more.

- Call on them when you chair meetings. They will welcome the "invitation" to speak.
- Give deserving women an opportunity to lead a project or sit on a committee.
- Give them visibility as conference speakers.

- Listen to them. Tom Marinelli, acting CEO of Ontario Lottery and Gaming, says he "grew up with three sisters" and understands that women communicate in a different way than men. But he learned to listen to his sisters, his wife, and daughter, and "that has made all the difference in my ability to listen to women. They can sometimes be overwhelmed by us [male leaders] . . . and so listening requires a more inclusive approach—one that will help us all, men *and* women."
- Give them an opportunity to develop and mentor other women.

Chapter Two

Silence the Inner Crow

I n her book *Addiction to Perfection,* psychoanalyst Marion Woodman tells us about an inner voice that repeatedly criticized her while she was writing her book. She calls this negative inner voice "the crow." As Woodman explains, "I have done battle with the black crow sitting on my left shoulder croaking, 'It isn't good enough. You haven't anything new to say. You don't say it well enough.'"[1] This inner crow seeks to undermine her sense of self as a writer.

Though not all of us are writers, women everywhere can share Woodman's familiarity with the crow that sits on our shoulder and croaks at us with negative self-talk. Before women can take the stage, they must confront this force—one of the most challenging aspects of our socialization.

At least 90 percent of the women who take our program immediately relate to the concept of a negative internal voice. We have a large statue of an ugly black crow in our firm's seminar room, and when we place it on the table, all the women say, "Oh yeah . . . the crow . . . It's in my mind all the time." They have their own version of this dark bird, but in every case that voice is continually cackling away in their mind with insults, taunts, and self-deprecating comments. Do you have an inner crow? Ask yourself, "When does it seem to plague you the most?" If we are to take the stage and speak as confident leaders, we must beat back the crow.

What the Inner Crow Says

It makes sense to depict this inner voice as a crow because of its loud, cawing sound and the negativity of its namesake. The expression "eat crow" refers to a situation in which one has humiliated oneself. Indeed, the crow in our minds does everything it can to embarrass and undermine us. Its insults sound like they're coming from our worst enemy or a critical parent.

As Arianna Huffington describes it in her book, *On Becoming Fearless,* "Imagine if someone invented a little tape recorder that we could attach to our brains to record everything we tell ourselves—a TiVo for our inner dialogue. What we'd discover is that not even our worst enemies talk about us the way we talk about ourselves. The negative self-talk starts as soon as we wake up—sometimes even before. . . . It's like having the world's worst roommate—one who's around 24/7."[2]

The following are just some of the things women we've worked with have told us about their mental cackling "crow."

- A financial planner making a presentation to colleagues hears, "You're going to fail. Not everyone in the room wants you to do well. They'll be thinking, 'She's done well up until now. Let's see if she can handle this or if she falls on her face.'"
- A managing director hears her crow say, "You're losing deals. You're such a failure."
- An executive returning to work after a maternity leave thinks, "Everyone will be scrutinizing my every move, wondering if I am up to the challenge. They'll be testing me, judging me, and looking for signs of fatigue."
- A CEO explains that she has the "Imposter Syndrome." The crow tells her, "You are in a position of power—but you don't belong there."
- A vice president of risk management for a global bank hears the crow tell her at meetings, "Keep your mouth shut. There are smarter and more senior people in this room than you."
- A project manager for a logistics company says that she frequently calls herself "stupid or silly," often out of frustration and even in front of her

children. She then worries, "Do I really want their primary female role model to be someone who considers herself stupid?"

These women have strong career paths; in some cases, they've risen to the top of the corporate ladder in their organizations. Clearly, the crow speaks to women at all levels, diminishing our sense of self-worth and becoming louder when we need to be stronger. And because it's an inner voice, outsiders rarely hear it. However, in our seminars the crow is often "exposed." One woman who was new to her company spoke up to tell the group about her own personal crow. Fighting back tears, she said to her boss, who was also in the seminar, "I feel constantly that I am letting you down, that I cannot give you what you want." And the boss replied, "I'm surprised. You are doing an excellent job."

Even famous women who appear super-confident have an "inner crow." Oscar-winning actress Anne Hathaway explains that "sometimes your brain gets caught up in the bulls—t and you wonder, 'Is that crew guy looking at me? Is he judging me? Did he work with someone better and is he now thinking about how much worse I am?'"[3]

Mandy-Rae Cruikshank, the world-famous diver who has gone deeper under water than any other woman, once described free diving as a mental battle with evil monkeys who rode on her shoulders, chattering destructive thoughts as she plunged deep into the ocean with only a face mask and the air in her lungs. "They can get to you," she said. "They say stuff like 'Whoa, you're really deep! You'll never make it! You're out of air, girl!' They want to freak you out."[4]

Marilyn Monroe had one of the most negative inner crows. She wrote down some of her memories and dreams, one of which was a nightmare in which her acting coach, Lee Strasberg, was a surgeon who was operating on her. When he opened her up, "there is absolutely nothing there—Strasberg is deeply disappointed." What's worse, "The only thing that came out was so finely cut sawdust—like out of a Raggedy Ann doll—and the sawdust spills all over the floor & table and Dr. H [her psychiatrist, assisting with the surgery] is puzzled because suddenly she realizes that this is a new type case. The patient . . . existing of complete emptiness." This dream dramatizes her crow's ugliest thoughts.[5]

The crow doesn't just belittle women's intelligence and professional ability. It also attacks their appearance. When we videotape women in our courses and have them watch the playback, we often hear them say, "Look how fat I am"; "That outfit doesn't suit me"; or "Wow, it's time for a face lift!" Why do we call attention to our age, our weight, and our flaws? There are a million ways we can make strong connections with our audience; putting ourselves down should never be one of them.

When women speak up at meetings, their inner crow is sitting right there on their shoulders. This evil bird might cackle, "Don't dare think of speaking up, not when you know so little about this subject," or "You aren't prepared." When you do summon the courage to speak up, the crow might admonish you, "That sounded stupid. What were you thinking? No wonder no one seems to have heard you." It's hard to be natural and relaxed when there's a bird of prey on your shoulder shouting orders.

And what professional woman with children has not heard the chiding voice of the crow lecture, "You should be home with your kids." I certainly know I did; it's a struggle to feel as though you're being a "good mom" while building a career. When I regularly delivered my son to school just as the assembly bell was ringing, my crow would be carping, "If you were a stay-at-home mom, you would get your kid to school on time."

Do men have an inner crow? According to Stephen Dyer, CFO of global agricultural firm Agrium, many do. After speaking to about forty women in his company, he said, "They were surprised when I told them that I've gone into roles as terrified as anybody who could possibly be taking on a new role. I did not feel that I could share this. And it was only four or five years ago that I shared my dyslexia, because I saw that as a weakness. We all have unique quirks—and it's important to let others know about them. If male leaders could share some of the fears they have had throughout their careers, it would go a long way in making women comfortable."

If men need to share more of their vulnerabilities, then women need to suppress their inner crow and give a lot less power to that nagging voice. Indeed, if we were to examine the gender differences between the female and male inner crows I suspect we'd find a louder and more constant cackling crow in women than in men.

How Can You Silence Your Inner Crow?

The crow is a wily beast, but it can be silenced if we put our minds to it! Let's look at five ways we can stop its heckling.

1. Become Aware of Its Presence

We ask participants in our women's seminar if they have an inner crow—and often receive a lively reaction that borders on a confessional. When I asked an audience of two hundred women, "Do you have an inner voice that tries to cut you down?" heads were nodding "yes" all over the room. We also have participants write down on a piece of paper the things their inner crows say to them. We tell them to be frank and not hold back—and then to crumple up that piece of paper as a symbol of the first step in exorcising the crow.

2. Don't Give Voice to Your Inner Crow

You might hear the crow—but you can take away its power by realizing that *no one else* hears its cawing. As one woman in our program told us, "You may think you're fat, or look in the mirror and say, 'Oh my god, look at that body!' But what you see is not an image that the rest of the world sees. Don't call attention to these negative self-perceptions." This woman—a banker—continues, "I used to have a boss who told me, 'The whole world doesn't need to know every slip-up.'" So, keep the crow to yourself. Don't ever undermine yourself in front of others. Eat crow if you have to; but don't share it! A good way to control the crow is to keep a journal of any negative-self talk, and make sure that each month you say fewer and fewer disparaging words about yourself. The goal is no journal entries!

3. Bolster Your Confidence

The crow feeds on our insecurities, so anything we do to bolster our confidence will diminish its power. Preparation is crucial here; as one woman, a regional executive for a logistics company, explained, "I have weekly calls with my senior leadership team. I used to be nervous about them and went in cold, without preparing anything. But now I actually take time to think about what I want to say. This eliminates some of the self-doubt and makes me more confident in those calls with my leadership team—and gives me the assurance to say to that crow, 'I'm not listening to you. This is all about *me* now.'" To achieve this mastery over the crow, prepare for key meetings, so you go in with a higher level of confidence.

4. Engage in Positive Self-Talk

Replace the crow's voice with your own confident inner voice by affirming that you have an important role. As one woman who was about to make a presentation on a project she had overseen told us, "Throughout the whole morning, I kept repeating to myself, 'I am the program manager, I am the program manager, I am the program manager.' I just nailed that into my head and got rid of that crow by replacing its voice with my own positive thoughts. I believe I did a great job." Another woman I worked with would go into every job interview or senior-level meeting saying to herself, "I am the vice president of marketing for one of the world's most successful technology companies." She repeated that mantra over and over again, and it gave her confidence by centering her on her area of expertise. Your self-talk may also be a moment of self-compassion in which you embrace your imperfection and vulnerability. As Christopher K. Germer, author of *The Mindful Path to Self-Compassion*, writes, "A moment of self-compassion like this can change your entire day. A string of such moments can change the course of your life."[6]

5. Defy the Inner Crow

When we become more daring, the crow will fly away—or at least become quieter. It realizes that its negative messages don't fit your behavior anymore. Chances are when you walk from your seat to the front of the boardroom, your crow is cackling, "I'm so nervous, they are not going to like anything I say." It's a negative message; how can you expect to get up there and greet everyone with a friendly, "Good morning!" Instead, you need to say to yourself as you walk to the front of the boardroom, "I am strong. I am powerful. This is the best presentation I have ever written and my audience is going to be blown away by what I have to say." That will enable you to go up there and start on a positive note.

Taking action against the crow may simply mean speaking up when it tells you that you have nothing to say, or asserting yourself when your inner voice tells you to be more passive. I was in a college class once with many young women who had attended prestigious prep schools and come from wealthy families. They spoke in class easily and often, seemingly without effort. I vowed that even though I came from a small town and a public high school, I would hold my own by *putting up my hand in every single class*. And that's exactly what I did. I forced myself to do it, even though I was trembling inside the moment before I raised my hand to answer a question or make a point. Gradually, though, the crow no longer held any sway over me—and I spoke with newfound confidence.

These five steps can silence your inner crow—which is critical, since this voice shapes the way *we think about ourselves*. We must banish those negatives if we want to communicate with confidence, strength, and authority—and build others' faith in our ability to do so. When we conquer the crow, we take control of our minds—and by doing so, we can give our full attention to taking the stage, and speaking with strength and authority.

Advice for Leaders of Women

Many women have a "cackling crow" in their minds telling them that they aren't good enough, or smart enough, or worthy enough. Women often describe their best bosses as those who "listen to my insecurities in a nonjudgmental way." You can help women strengthen their self-esteem and become stronger contributors in the following ways:

- When they put themselves down, don't take such comments at face value. Recognize their negative self-talk as an externalization of fears and anxieties.

- Take them aside and encourage them not to put themselves down, because it undermines people's confidence in them. Use this coaching moment to reinforce something positive about them.
- Help them find their own "voices" by asking them for ideas, thoughts, and feelings about an issue, problem, or challenge.
- Share your own insecurities—make women feel they are not alone.

Chapter Three

Develop a Center Stage Mindset

I know an HR leader who'd been with a global technology firm for twenty years and had been in the "talent pool" for ten long years. She worked her way up the ladder to the director level, and was waiting for her next big move when her progress stalled. Her performance reviews were first rate, and her boss regularly complimented her on her work—but no promotion. She was distressed that she hadn't moved up to senior management.

It became clear to me as I listened to her account that much of the problem rested with her own motivation. In fact, she recently had an opportunity for a significant promotion but turned it down. Why? "My boss told me he couldn't do without me," she explained. "Besides, it was just before the Christmas holidays, and I just couldn't think about it with all the shopping to do." No wonder she hadn't advanced in ten long years. Can you imagine a male not going for a promotion because he had shopping to do? Or because his boss needed him? This real-life story illustrates a sad truth: moving ahead often is not about external obstacles. If you want to succeed you must develop an absolute determination to succeed—a center stage mindset. There are several steps that will enable you to do so.

Step 1: Know You *Deserve* the Spotlight

The first thing is to believe you deserve to be in the limelight. One female investment banker told me, "Most of our clients are men in the hedge fund industry, and they're competitive. I take the approach that I deserve to have a seat at their table." Margaret Thatcher—one of the most powerful women in the Western world—also felt she deserved a place on stage. At the tender age of nine she won a poetry reading prize at a local drama festival and when her headmistress said, "You were lucky Margaret!" she replied, "I wasn't lucky, I deserved it."[1] In our women's course we ask participants, "How many of you were the girl in high school or grade school who always had her hand up and knew the answers?" Usually three-quarters of the women in the room go "That was me!" Yet these same women tell us that when their CEO or another senior executive comes to meet with them and asks them, "What do you think about this or that issue?" they respond with silence. They still deserve to be in the limelight! Knowing you deserve a place on stage is critical to your career success.

Step 2: Seize Opportunities to Shine

Once you are on stage, take every chance you can to shine. A recent study by IBM entitled *Your Journey to Executive* surveyed 639 female IBM executives from thirty countries. Based on the feedback, study authors Heather Howell and Kim Stephens state, "High performance is essential, but not enough. To succeed to the executive ranks, you have to be visible. You have to be willing to take on critical, visible roles that stretch you, develop you and provide an opportunity to demonstrate competence and leadership."[2]

I asked former Intel CEO Craig Barrett when I met him at a conference some years ago, "What will enable women to get ahead in companies like Intel?" He immediately responded, "They should put their hand up, take that next job, that next project; they don't do that enough."[3] Similarly, Richard Nesbitt, CEO of CIBC World Markets, encourages women to "tell your boss that you want to sit on a committee, tell your boss that you want a new project to demonstrate that you're capable of doing more than you're doing, and tell your boss what job you want next. You don't need to have a long-term career plan, but you should know what the next step is. The most important thing for women is striving to advance—however that might be in a person's individual circumstance."

Those who lead, sponsor, and mentor women also have a strong role to play in helping them seize opportunities. A friend of mine named Cathryn told me how her boss had given her an opportunity to shine on stage.

> I was a new SVP who just moved to New York City for my first "big" job working for a reputable financial services firm. I had only been there twelve weeks when my EVP (human resources) boss called me the night before the annual all-company meeting to tell me he was deathly ill and had lost his voice. He said, "I need you to deliver my presentation tomorrow." I had no time to contemplate or listen to my inner crow, so I simply said, "Okay, I've got it covered." I did not realize until later that I was preceding a very popular CEO and if the presentation did not go well, it could be career-limiting. I was also told that twenty thousand employees from all over the country would be attending live or via video link. No pressure! My fifteen minutes of "fame" was fleeting but the presentation was a huge success. By speaking from my heart—and covering necessary content—I gained instant credibility as a leader. Employees—and executive management—came to see me as someone they could trust.

In the same vein, women should seize opportunities to make bold career moves. Men seem to naturally do this—whereas women often hold back. A spokesperson for a major bank observed, "Women are not as aggressive as men in actively searching for the next job. Women only look for a job when they need one. Men are always looking for a job. There are an equal number of men and women who say they would like a top job. But the difference is that women don't think they'll get those top jobs, so they don't try for them. Men start talking about their next bonus the day after they receive their current one; women wait until their bonus is paid and talk about the bonus they've just received.

They'll say, 'Oh thanks for this.' Women are grateful; men are ambitious. Women focus on what they've just been given. Men focus on what they want next."

Seizing career opportunities involves showing the world that you are a capable, ambitious leader. Moya Greene, CEO of Britain's Royal Mail, says, "Ambition is not a four letter word. . . . Women have to want the job and not treat ambition as something they should hide."[4] You won't have a successful career unless you know where you want to go. In short, you must have a clear, single-minded intention to seize opportunities. One woman named Lucille told me, "There is a possibility of a new department being set up and I feel I'm the right person to lead that new unit. The 'old Lucille' [pre–Taking the Stage] would have thought, 'I hope they pick me.' The new one is determined to get it." Pull out all the stops when you go for a new position or assignment, and sell yourself vigorously. Don't say, "I *think* I could do the work." Let them know you absolutely can achieve what's expected in that role.

Few of us can create an exact roadmap of where we want to go. Nor should you feel you have to. There are too many chance events, opportunities that appear out of the blue, and you must seize them in an instant. But have a main objective that will guide you through your own career and give you the drive, passion, and dedication so necessary to career success.

I didn't map out my path with precision; in fact there was a serendipity about my career. The one constant was my ambition—and the means of realizing it was communications. I always knew that I wanted my career to "add up" to something meaningful—I wanted to make a strong contribution. My mother was the force in my life who made me realize this was possible. She used to say to me, "Do something great with your life." She instilled in me a drive that has infused my career, despite the twists and turns this path has taken.

Simply let your ambition drive you to greater and greater heights by seizing opportunities as they come to you. You'll feel a push when it's time to move on that will help you identify your next big opportunity. Indeed, one senior executive I interviewed said that "organizations often have no idea what they want to do with you; so it's important to stake out your next move and let your boss and others know what that is."

Step 3: Don't Retreat to the Wings

If there is a formula for staying on center stage it is refusing to be sidelined or satisfied when you hit a "wall." As one graduate of Taking the Stage said, "You just feel sometimes that people expect you to stay where you are because you are close to retirement. But even though I just had my 'big sixtieth,' I hear there is a controller position coming up—and I'll be applying for it."

The most common reason women give for moving "off stage" is their personal or family life. There's no one right answer here. For many women, and some men, long days in the office and career success appear less desirable than spending time at home, especially when small children are involved. This decision is up to each woman. Any course of action involves sacrifices and rewards. Still, if women want to stay on stage, as they wrestle with this challenge they must think beyond the traditional roles and make deliberate choices that may involve less time with children, partners, or parents. If you don't make these choices, you may end up wondering, "Where did my career go?"

When I was eight months pregnant with my first child and had just left university teaching, it would have been a perfect time to say, "I'm dropping out of the workforce for a while." But I didn't want a hiatus in my career, so I interviewed for a job—looking as big as a barn in my full-term maternity outfit. I remember feeling hot and overwhelmed by the pressure I was under from the aggressive interviewer. Nevertheless, I got the job—the offer came the day my son was born—and I went to work eight weeks later in a position that gave me entrance to an exciting career in corporate communications. I was thrilled that I'd made it into a new world where my career could take off!

This professional focus is critical for women who want a strong career track. That decision was incredibly difficult for me, as were countless other things. I wasn't there to see my child take his first steps. Dressing in the dark when the baby was asleep led to a few wardrobe malfunctions. And our succession of six nannies was not easy on me—they were all high maintenance. One of them wore low-cut tops and high-cut shorts, and was in the process of making my husband a bathrobe when I fired her! But everything worked out. That baby boy is my successor in The Humphrey

Group—and is now the CEO of the company that I founded. Yes—building your career while building a family is a messy process; but the alternatives, at least for me, were not as desirable, and they may not be for many of you.

Don't let anything drive you into the wings. Think of center stage as your rightful place, and do everything you can to stay there. Developing a leader's mindset is a crucial step that involves knowing you deserve to be on stage, seizing opportunities to shine, and not retreating in the face of challenges. It can be difficult to get the home/work balance right. But don't let it destabilize your career—or family. Your center stage mindset will provide your all-important sense of direction.

Advice for Leaders of Women

Women often need encouragement to move into "center stage"—and commit fully to their careers. You can help them make this shift.

- Encourage them to take more risks in their careers and get beyond the "I can't take this on because . . ." line of reasoning.
- *Never* be the reason they give up an opportunity—as in "My boss needs me, so I'll pass on that career move." Help them be "selfish" rather than "selfless" when it comes to their careers.
- Beware of making assumptions that would backburner women, as in "She has a young family, so she would never be interested in this international assignment."
- Don't feel that conversations about work/life balance are off limits to you as a leader of women. Discuss this issue openly and supportively with the women who report to you. No one should judge another person's choices. But make it attractive for women to commit to work, return to work after maternity leave, and grow with your firm.

Chapter Four

Speak Up Confidently

A young Canadian female engineer was participating in a company-wide training exercise on "Nuclear Safety Culture for Managers." Toward the end, each table of attendees was asked to share their findings with the entire room. The young woman's tablemates nominated her to present their observations. She stood up and spoke eloquently about the importance of safety standards for nuclear reactors. What was even more exciting was that (in her words), "Right in the middle of presenting, I suddenly realized that I was talking about nuclear safety to the *chief engineer* and I was comfortable holding my ground. This was the 'aha' moment that showed me I had taken the stage."

Speaking up is an imperative for women who wish to move forward in their careers. As John Montalbano, CEO of RBC Global Asset Management, told me, "What is most critical for women is having the confidence to speak in formal situations, such as an operating committee meeting or a board meeting. Among many things, leaders are chosen based on their contributions in group settings—something that's critical in developing confidence among your peers. If you are a leader, you are first among equals. So you will need to build your peers' confidence if you want their support." In other words, if you don't speak up, no one will know what you think or how bright you are. They'll often assume you have nothing to say!

But speaking up is not easy for many women (and for some men). Agrium CFO Steve Dyer sums it up well: "Women tend to sit back more than men. They are not truly at the table in terms of feeling comfortable putting forward ideas and making comments or suggestions. Men tend to be more aggressive and assertive than women. It doesn't mean that women don't have the same quality of ideas. . . . It's just that women need an environment in which they are *encouraged* to bring forward their ideas within an organization." Hopefully, more organizations and senior leaders will create such an atmosphere. But it is also women's responsibility to find that encouragement within themselves—and to speak up with courage and confidence. The answer is to bolster your confidence by internalizing the following speaking strategies that provide a strong foundation for speaking up.

Show Up

The starting point of speaking up is showing up. This can mean taking time to attend a networking event, setting up a meeting with a mentor or sponsor, putting yourself forward for a new job, or creating face time with your boss or CEO. We observe again and again that women just don't take the initiative to be present. In one high-tech firm we worked with, not a single woman showed up at a networking session with the CEO! In another instance, a female director told me with regret why a male colleague was promoted before she was. He set up monthly meetings with his boss's boss to "brief" him, whereas she focused simply on her work and stayed behind the scenes.

Reaching out is not easy, even for high-profile leaders. Yahoo CEO Marissa Mayer is by her own account very shy and has had to force herself to attend informal gatherings. She explains that for the first fifteen minutes, she just wants to leave. But she'll look at her watch and tell herself, "You can't leave until time x."[1] She finds that if she makes herself stay for a given period, she'll begin enjoying the event and the conversation.

Showing up means putting yourself out there. Think of all those interviews, meetings, and social events that seem to accomplish little as a chance to raise your profile and enhance your confidence. Not only are you sending a positive message when you attend such events, but you are also gaining access to "powerful others."

Prepare, Prepare, Prepare

People generally think of *preparing* as something they do for formal events—getting a PowerPoint deck in order, or planning a meeting agenda. Of course, you absolutely want to prepare for major presentations. But you also have to prepare for informal events. A public relations manager said, "I'm a very talkative, relaxed, and easygoing person, which I thought worked for me. But I have learned that I should prepare for informal meetings. We have a department meeting every week and I now think, 'Here are the three things that I want to talk about and then I highlight what they are.'" A banker similarly said: "Before taking your program, I'd say whatever was at the top of my head about my field when I walked into a meeting. Now when I drive to work in the morning, I think, 'What do I want to tell my colleagues? Something about a particular client? An opportunity?' I really think it through."

You must also prepare for "spontaneous" exchanges. The elevator conversation is a perfect example of an impromptu encounter that demands forethought. I'll often coach private clients on how to talk with their executives during a chance meeting at 8 a.m. when they are both getting their coffee. It's easy to simply blurt out something generic like, "What terrible weather we're having" if you aren't prepared. But planning in advance will give you an extraordinary amount of confidence, because you will know exactly what to say, whatever the situation. For example, if you know your head of sales was on a business trip abroad, think ahead to ask him, "Was your trip productive?" Or "Tell me about the new clients you met." Such questions will show that you are committed to the business, and it will give the executive a chance to open up.

Prepare, too, for networking events so you can make the most of these opportunities. Find out who is going to be there and whom you want to talk to. Prepare to speak intelligently about what *they* care about. One human resource executive explained to me, "Networking has to be about the other person—a big mistake people make about networking is that they think it is about them. Sure, be prepared to talk about yourself. But if you are attending a networking event, find out all you can about the other people you may wish to talk to. If you do this, then you can say, 'I found this very interesting article, and I'll send it to you,' or 'I saw your name in the newspaper for a promotion. Congratulations.'" Women are not always good at taking information and delivering it as an action item in an encounter. Use such information to build a relationship.

Listen . . . to Others and to Yourself

Listening is also a critical part of speaking up with confidence, and women are generally superb listeners. In her *Harvard Business Review* article "Ways Women Lead," Judy Rosener notes that women typically "encourage participation and share power and information."[2] That's a strength, but at the same time as we listen to *others* we must not lose sight of what *we* think or have to say. Know how to move from what you've heard to what you want to say. Ask yourself as someone is speaking, "Do I agree?" "Do I see a solution?" "How can I build upon what's been said?" Figuring out these answers will allow you to speak up and make a contribution. You'll be able to segue smoothly from the other person's point to yours.

Sumittra, an HR director in Thailand, shared with us how she had learned the importance of staying in touch with her own thinking while she was listening.

> In situations where I am listening, I often get excited and run out of words to defend my thoughts. I tend to give in and go with the conclusion of the discussion even though I am not convinced. After attending your course, I had a disagreement with a male colleague. During the discussion, I listened carefully and reminded myself to hear his point of view and maintain my own critical judgement about what he was saying. I stayed calm and developed in my mind a key message about our areas of agreement. Then I gave him my professional opinion on what I thought was the right thing for the company and reminded him of the difficult decision we both needed to make. In the end, we worked as a team to find the most appropriate solutions.

This story provides an excellent lesson whether you are listening to one person or to a group discussion. As you listen, stay calm, and keep the two "tracks" of thinking in mind—theirs and yours. Think of it as "listening in stereo"! By listening in this collaborative way, you can take the discussion to the next level, provide solutions to problems, responses to challenges, and outcomes that reflect shared goals. When you do this, you will be speaking up confidently.

Speak with Substance

If you want others to listen to you, make sure whatever you say has substance. As John Montalbano explains, "Most organizations in today's competitive world are meritocracies. To stand out from the crowd, you have to do a good job of articulating how your efforts have contributed to the organization's success and express a keenness to build on that success. Key people need to know how your specific efforts have led to positive outcomes for the organization."

You impart this kind of substance when you share ideas about organization-wide accomplishment. Women too often focus on their work; and although this seems to validate them, it can turn off their audiences. Present strong, clear, high-level messages, and people will listen.

And, *don't be afraid* to speak with substance—sounding bright, capable, and intellectually savvy is your right. One senior executive told me that a high-ranking woman on his team "dumbs herself down. She wants people to like her, not be threatened by her." This is a huge handicap for some women—wanting to be liked at the expense of making a serious contribution to discussions. Playing dumb will get you nowhere in today's organizations that rely on smart people to speak with substance.

Develop a Political "Sixth Sense"

It can be intimidating—for both women and men—to have senior people in the room. But if you know how to communicate your messages to the right people in a politically astute way, you can raise your profile and gain respect.

A lot of men seem to have an innate political consciousness—likely because they are part of the political structure, the hierarchy. It's their world, and they are comfortable with it. But women often feel like outsiders in the political structure. They frequently develop relationships based on whom they *like*, not who holds power. Many more women than men tell us that acting politically makes them feel insincere. One woman remarked, "I can't suck up or manage upward. I don't want to spend time building relationships with senior management just to make myself look good. I see managing up as self-promotional. I'd rather spend time helping my team get things done. Managing below is accomplishing things." While an understandable point of view, this attitude is a death wish.

To begin with, it's crucial to know who the powerful people in your organization are. "Our organization," says a female director, "is *loaded* with politics." Being politically intelligent means identifying the top decision makers—as well as the people who influence them. It means knowing who to go to for help if you're in trouble.

As an exercise, think of the five people in your organization who are essential to your success. Now, identify the status of each of those relationships as being one of the following: in its *infancy*, *established*, or *strong*. Finally, determine what action you need to take next to help advance each of those relationships. Let's suppose you have just joined the firm, and you know that your boss's boss is one of the five key people on your horizon, and your relationship with him is in its *infancy*. You might ask your boss if she will arrange for you to meet with her boss, the executive vice president, once a month. Explain how critical it will be for you to brief the EVP on the work you are doing and how it will benefit the department. Take those steps, and you will be speaking up in a way that moves your career forward. And don't rule out executive assistants and coaches who work with the executives as key people for you.

View every situation as an opportunity to cement relationships with people at the top. Whether you're at a management meeting or a social event, focus on those high-ranking people. View any forum where several executives are present as a golden opportunity. Sit near them. Many women often sit as far from executives as possible at the boardroom table; these women feel more comfortable with people they know. But to advance, don't hang out with your old friends or close colleagues. You need to figure out how to break new ground with senior officers whenever you can. By sitting where the power is, you give yourself authority.

Follow one senior woman's advice: "Be aware of your senior organization. Try to know as much about people at that level as you can—what they're passionate about in terms of the company's goals, and what they don't like." And when you speak up, do so in such a way that you connect with what they believe is important. In so doing, you will earn their respect and gain confidence.

Be Direct

Speaking up confidently also means learning to be direct. Because women often want to be liked, they say things to get approval and avoid saying things that will be challenged. But being liked is not as important as being respected. Don't look for love in the boardroom! To be a confident communicator, speak with conviction and go against the grain if necessary.

Express ideas you feel will contribute to the dialogue, even when they challenge others in the room. Men are good at this. As one woman said, "In my company the challenging comments usually come from men. They realize that it's a way to get noticed at the senior executive level. Men do this really well. They don't care if the executive challenges them back, whereas women take this personally. And men get reinforced by doing this. They see it as acting responsibly. But we regard it negatively as challenging authority."

Directness is important whether you are talking "down" or "up" the ladder. Women can be so caring when talking to their staff that they soften what they say—and thereby risk having a team member not hear their message. They might do the same when they talk upward because they worry about alienating those in power. But the consequence is just as significant: others don't perceive them as credible. Follow the advice of one female senior banker: "I have to give CEOs 'the truth' all the time. I'll say, 'There are certain shareholders who don't believe the guidance you are giving. They are worried that you're too aggressive with your numbers. And you need to address that!' That's my job—to tell them the truth." JP Morgan Chase chairman and CEO Jamie Dimon paid a high compliment to Ina Drew, the firm's former chief investment officer, when he said about her, "If I had a bad idea, she'd tell me it was a bad idea. She had her opinion. She was strong."[3]

When Hewlett-Packard CEO Meg Whitman challenged authority, it certainly didn't hurt her career. Whitman was a junior partner at Bain Consulting when she asked her CEO, Tom Tierney, if he wanted staff feedback about his leadership style. After he nodded "yes," she drew a picture of a steamroller on a whiteboard. "This is you, Tom," she said. "You're too pushy—you're not letting us build consensus leadership." Tierney was taken aback, but later said he respected her for speaking that way and he did tone down his style. He also said the conversation "left me liking Meg more."[4]

The fundamentals discussed in this chapter will serve you well and will give you the confidence to speak up. And as you do, you will have a higher profile, advance your career, and make a strong contribution to your company.

Advice for Leaders of Women

Speaking up confidently is an imperative for both men and women; but as this chapter suggests, women face more challenges to becoming confident speakers than men do. There are many things you can do to "bring them along."

- Before meetings, ask women to think about the subject and let them know you will want to hear their thoughts and ideas.
- In meetings, draw them into the discussion. Remember that many women tend to wait "in the wings" until invited to participate. Once you do so, your female leaders will likely speak up more frequently.
- Establish a team atmosphere in meetings by providing a level of comfort and inclusiveness. Even leaders can get caught up in the heat of the moment and forget to bring everybody along.
- If a woman has made a good point, reinforce it. Women in particular need such support.

Chapter Five

Be Assertive, Not Aggressive

I was recently honored at a dinner for my role in building The Humphrey Group. All evening employees, clients, family, and friends delivered toasts and accolades telling stories of my entrepreneurship. Then, at the end of the event, a friend went up to the front of the room and stunned me by telling the audience, "I have known Judith longer than any of you have, and she is the most *aggressive* woman I know." This came like a thunderbolt, particularly because this individual was a longtime friend. And though she meant it as a compliment, it fits with the fact that people—both men and women—often stereotype women as "aggressive" when they have asserted themselves in some way—in their careers or their personal lives.

There is a big difference between being assertive and being aggressive. It's important to know the difference. Assertiveness is an expression of confidence; it is self-affirming. It shows your conviction about yourself and your ideas. It's a crucial quality to have if you want to take the stage. Aggressiveness—which derives from the Latin word *aggressio*, meaning "attack"—literally means "going on the attack." Being aggressive involves confrontational behavior, and it's counterproductive. Ultimately it closes doors rather than opening them. So, as you take the stage, it's important to do so in a way that is assertive, not aggressive.

If you are on the right side of this dichotomy, you will be better able to build relationships, win over your audiences, and succeed in your career.

Assertive Women Are Often Perceived as Aggressive

Although it's true some women are "bossy" or aggressive, females are tarred with this brush far more often than males are. To illustrate this point, Facebook COO and *Lean In* author Sheryl Sandberg regularly asks her audiences for a show of hands to indicate how often the individuals in the room have been accused of overly aggressive behavior in the workplace. She says that "very few men ever raise their hands on that question." But hundreds of hands go up when she asks women that same question.[1]

Why are women so frequently accused of aggressiveness? It's largely a result of stereotyping. When women move out of "nice" and become more assertive, they are seen as "aggressive," "bossy," "bitchy," "emotional," or "pushy." More than one senior executive has complained to me: "We have some women around here who exhibit more aggressive behavior than men do. I don't know why they do what they do, but they can be extremely aggressive." In contrast, in the past twenty-five years, I have *never* heard a single senior executive complain about men being too aggressive.

Such attitudes help explain why women are viewed as less than ideal bosses. A recent Gallup poll indicated that both males and females would prefer to work for a male boss. Thirty-five percent of the people polled prefer to have a man in charge, whereas only 23 percent prefer to have a woman in charge. Significantly, though, the gap has been closing since 1953, when this question was first asked. At that time the poll indicated that 66 percent favored male bosses and only five percent preferred female bosses.[2]

Don't Worry About Being Called Bossy

Responding negatively to being labeled bossy, aggressive, or pushy will not serve you well, and it won't necessarily change people's language patterns. You may well be called these names if you are a self-confident, assertive leader. We've seen how the charge of being bossy is hurled at women more often than at men. But going on the attack is not the answer, nor is going silent or being devious to avoid these labels. As Arianna Huffington writes in her book *On Becoming Fearless*, "We so want to be liked that we worry about alienating people, so we often try to get what we want behind the scenes. . . . It's nice to be nice, but it can be extremely draining and self-destructive when it mutes our voice."[3] Accept the fact, as Sheryl Sandberg remarks, that being labeled as bossy is simply a reference to our executive leadership skills.[4] Take it as a compliment! But don't use these labels to describe yourself, other women, or young girls. I once saw a T-shirt a little girl was wearing, and on it were printed in bright colors words like *bossy*. How long will it be before she calls herself bossy?

So remember: Being called "aggressive," "bossy," or "bitch" is not your fault—or your problem. Although we'd rather be given more attractive labels, realize that these stereotypes are simply the world's way of classifying you as strong.

Avoid Aggressiveness; It Doesn't Work for Women *or* Men

You still want to take care not to become aggressive as you develop into a stronger leader. The warning signs are clear: this kind of behavior involves anger, emotionalism, and personal attacks. Whatever short-term gains you might seem to reap from these outbursts, they are an unproductive approach for any woman (or man) who wants to take the stage. If such behavior is part of your repertoire, get rid of it.

Although aggression is never right—and being assertive almost always is—there are understandable reasons why some women show signs of anger and edginess in the workplace. When a woman becomes frustrated at being interrupted, not being heard, or not being taken seriously, she may raise her voice and sound aggressive. Indeed, a woman's inner dialogue might sound something like this: "No one ever listens to me! Well, this time they are going to—even if I have to ram it down their throats." As one of our instructors said to me, "I sometimes find a hidden aggression in women partly because their way of doing things is not being understood." Speaking in a male-dominated culture is often not easy for women, and assertiveness can easily turn into aggressiveness.

Women understandably grow restless with male behaviors they cannot relate to. For example, one female executive said, "I find that men just talk for the sake of talking. I'm here, so I need to say *something*. They just pontificate." This can be disturbing, because women often view this gamesmanship as over-the-top or insincere. As a result, they shut down in some cases; in others, they may go on the attack and become aggressive or shrill.

Sometimes a woman may feel upset and slip into a passive-aggressive mode. Take the following role play from one of our seminars:

> Valerie came to us and said, "I am fed up with men who interrupt and hijack me when I am presenting." She said she tried to get louder when they did so, but then they got even louder. Our instructor suggested that she tell her audience at the beginning of her presentation that they should save their questions and comments to the end. But she became passive-aggressive as she attempted to role play how she would do that, saying, "Pleeeeeeeeeeease. I'm going to finish what I have to say and I don't want any interruptions." Her language and delivery were dripping with annoyance, and her tone was peevish and irritable. Her eyebrows were furrowed, and her chin was jutting forward and her lips pursed.

Women can also develop the rough edges of the organizations or departments they find themselves in. As one of our senior female clients said, "I was an auditor and had staff working for me, and the men would come back into the office crying because the CEO yelled at them. So I would have to deal with the CEO myself, and I had to adopt his tone if he was going to take me seriously."

My first job was in a hard-driving technology company. Even though my boss was a great mentor, he often vented his anger at me and others. I frequently left his office nearly in tears—and I was far from a pushover. Everyone stayed silent in staff meetings for fear of being attacked. Too many organizations deem this aggressive behavior as acceptable; occasionally, it's even admired, as when employees swap "war stories." But it shouldn't be. It doesn't work for leaders, it alienates subordinates, and it hurts loyalty and productivity.

Respond to aggressiveness by being assertive—or as chapter 8 discusses, by "holding your ground." Don't become emotional, angry, frustrated, or aggressive back. Much of this book can be read as a guidebook on assertiveness. Although every section focuses on a particular area, it suggests how to develop this quality—from resolving to take the stage to creating strong scripts, strengthening the power of your voice, and developing a leadership presence.

Women have been suffering under the burden of being called aggressive for a long time. It's often an unfair label and applied indiscriminately to self-confident females. Don't let such name-calling put you off your game. But at the same time, make sure you don't *develop* those negative qualities. Let's all—women and men—move to a higher plane. I am reminded of the title of a book by Debra Benton about senior executives. It's called *Lions Don't Need to Roar*.[5] Although that book was published in 1992, its advice has never been timelier. We all need to work together to create an atmosphere of assertiveness, and shun aggressiveness—or labeling others as aggressive—so we can be better leaders for the future.

Advice for Leaders of Women

Often, "aggressive" is in the eye of the beholder—and women are accused of being aggressive when they are only being assertive. As a result, many women are reluctant to be assertive for fear that others will label them as too strong. You can help your organization develop confident, assertive women.

- Be a role model yourself. Show women what assertiveness looks like and show others how to reinforce assertiveness in the workplace.
- Encourage both men and women in your organization to shed the aggressive style that was more appropriate to top-down command-and-control organizations.

- Don't allow anyone in your organization to refer to women as "bossy," "pushy," or "aggressive."
- Help women become more assertive by saying, "Let's hear what Vanessa has to say about that," or "That's Jocelyn's area of expertise—let's let her speak."
- Commend women for their assertiveness, particularly in meetings and discussions where peers and colleagues are present.

Chapter Six

Promote Yourself

M y husband jokingly says that if I ever write an autobiography, it should be called *Always Selling*. As a young girl, I remember going door to door in our small New England town, selling packets of seeds, greeting cards, and potholders I had made on a small loom. Sure, I was scared when I rang each doorbell, looking up at the little window in the door where a woman peered out to see who was knocking. I gulped when I saw her face. But once she opened the door, somehow I knew it would be worth it. I walked away from each encounter with something—not always a sale, but often with a cup of hot chocolate, some kind words, and most important a heightened sense of self-worth. Everybody took me seriously when I was selling!

In today's corporate world, few skills are more important than putting yourself forward so you can gain attention and respect from others. Catalyst's study, "The Myth of the Ideal Worker," shows that "when women were most proactive in making their achievements visible, they advanced further, were more satisfied with their careers, and had greater compensation growth than women who were less focused on calling attention to their successes."[1] This insight makes clear that women should make the leap from caution and humility to risk taking and self-promotion.

An Appetite for Humble Pie

A *New York Times* article notes that "SELF-PROMOTION is another crucial skill for those intent on moving up, but women are more likely to consider such behavior unseemly."[2] Our taste for humility goes back to our upbringing, when we worried that others would misconstrue pride in our accomplishments as conceit or vanity. One woman told us that she well remembers going through grade school and having a classmate say, "Smarty pants—you think you're so good" and hearing "Stop showing off" from her parents and teachers. In many cases, we still program girls to tone down. Even mothers who want to be successful themselves often encourage humility in their daughters. Those in our Taking the Stage seminars regularly have "aha" moments when they discover that they are programming their daughters to be quiet and humble. A woman said, "Every day I tell my little girl to stop showing off, and to be more polite. I tell her she talks too much. And most horribly, I tell her that she should keep her accomplishments to herself so that she doesn't make other people feel bad. This course has not only changed my life; it has changed hers."

As a result of our upbringing, women promote themselves less than men do. Neena, who works in a capital markets organization, said, "Males aren't afraid to brag about what they've done. But females usually stay quiet." Too often women hide their own accomplishments while lauding their team's contributions. One woman explained, "I was hesitant to toot my own horn, and quick to give kudos to my team. That's how I led them or motivated them." As Peggy Klaus writes in her book, *Brag!*, "Women are less likely to draw attention to themselves and take ownership of their successes. They tend to attribute their accomplishments to other people, their families, or a work team. That's all very nice, but it's those who visibly take credit for accomplishments who are rewarded with promotions and gem assignments."[3]

How to Promote Yourself

Self-promotion may not come naturally for many women. But we can work on it until it becomes second nature. As one young woman put it,

"I used to think it was a great quality to be modest. But I now realize that I can promote myself in a very matter-of-fact way. It just means speaking the truth about my strengths and abilities." Selling your strengths is a day-in-and-day-out process that will take you into the spotlight and keep you there, not only in meetings, but in your career and life. Here are the fundamentals to keep in mind when you make a case for yourself.

Know What It Is . . . and Isn't

To begin with, know exactly what "self-promotion" means. When you discuss your accomplishments, do so based on substance and show how they promote the goals of your organization. For example, you might say, "I was pleased to lead the team on this project, and am delighted with the response of our internal partners." Such salesmanship is in the interest of everyone—you, your company, and your stakeholders. To become a successful self-promoter you must be able to articulate your value in a way that shows a contribution to your organization or to others who are in the room. Your value in this broader sense must be clearly apparent to everyone involved.

Promoting yourself *does not mean* narrowly focusing on your own personal brand—or boasting in the "ME, ME, ME" sense. Self-aggrandizement is never a good thing. It's important to avoid anything that smacks of a focus on you alone. For example, you would not say, "I completed that project myself." This kind of statement isolates you and goes against the idea of being a team player. You could, however, say, "My presentation went really well." But even better would be, "My presentation went really well and the client loves what we have to offer." In short, trumpet the contributions you are making to others . . . to the firm . . . to the audience . . . to the client . . . to the world.

Be Motivated!

When you engage in this carefully orchestrated self-promotion, you must be highly motivated, especially if self-promotion takes you outside your comfort zone. Every time you walk into a room, attend a meeting, sit at the table, or have a business conversation, ask yourself, "What do I want out of this meeting?" A promotion? A leadership opportunity? A chance to be heard? An opportunity to make our company or department look good in the eyes of a customer? A stronger partnership with an internal partner? Acceptance for an idea or proposal? The list is endless.

You don't want to go out of that room empty-handed. You must be hungry for success, whether that represents a commitment from a customer, approval from your boss, or an offer of a new position. Staying focused on exactly what you want from that encounter will push you to put yourself forward. This mindset is necessary for both men and women; once you have identified what you want, you will have a reason to advance your case.

Know What You're Selling

To promote yourself, you'll need to have your successes top-of-mind. I urge women to keep a book of their accomplishments. This will encourage you to take note of your achievements and acknowledge them in conversation. List your successes, such as "I completed the pilot project with great feedback from all parties!" Then when someone compliments you, you'll say "Thank you, I am proud of that" rather than "it was nothing."

This self-promotion is easier said than done. Even when the world tells us that we have achieved something great, it is often difficult for us to accept those accolades. I remember one client, the head of a biotech firm, who was receiving an award for all the things she had done to contribute to her industry—nurturing young talent, supporting startup firms, serving as a mentor, and leading a strong midsized company.

She was justifiably proud of this award. But her PR rep told me she was uncomfortable in the spotlight, and I saw that for myself when we worked together on her speech. When I presented her with the first draft she said, "It isn't me. It sounds like gee whiz aren't I wonderful." In the second draft I focused less on her achievements and emphasized her feeling of pride. "I am proud . . ." was the refrain of that version. Still, she said, it is "too much about me." The third draft, at her request, praised others around her—family, employees, industry colleagues. The message now was, "I accept this award on behalf of so many people around me." After reading it out loud, she said it still sounded "too boastful," so she asked me to "tone it down further." I didn't know how I could tone it down without eliminating her entirely! In the end, the fourth (and final) draft presented the theme she felt was best: "I feel lucky." She asked me what to wear and said she thought she should dress down, perhaps a simple black cocktail dress, because she didn't want to draw too much attention to herself.

When the big night came, she enjoyed the event, brought her family up on stage, and paid tribute to the world for bringing this "luck" to her. She was gracious, lovely, and recognized by the industry. This story has stayed with me because I know she and other women need to be more comfortable singing their own praises. It was a huge effort for her to speak about her success, as it is for so many women. We need to know that it's okay to sell ourselves, okay to speak about what we have done. Our accomplishments are not the result of blind luck. This ability to know *what in ourselves* we are selling is something we need to practice every day. Otherwise, when we are at meetings, on the phone, or in the elevator, we won't mention those accomplishments, and when others do, we will dismiss them.

Learn to Brag

You can begin to practice bragging in "safe" situations—perhaps at home or in the classroom. In our seminars we ask women to boast by telling them, "Go to an extreme. Brag your face off." This makes many women so uncomfortable that we have to show them what it might sound like. When they think they're being extreme in their bragging and are blushing with embarrassment, they usually have just begun to reach the tone and content to project balanced self-esteem. Our conditioning is *that strong*.

This is not to say that these women don't think they have made brilliant contributions or submitted fabulous reports. They just can't seem to tell the world about it without excruciating discomfort. They'd prefer that others guess how great they are. We ask them to write down three brags and read them to the group. For example, our instructor might have them write out three statements about themselves, and tell them to "Begin each sentence with a superlative like 'I'm great at . . .' Or 'I'm fantastic at . . .' Or 'There's no one better than I am at . . .'" The fascinating thing about this exercise is how difficult it is. We've seen women blush and squirm in their chairs at having to compliment themselves. Of course, words like "I'm fantastic" would not be used in a business situation, but getting women to even speak these words centers them in a way that is important if they are going to promote themselves.

The following is a transcript from one of our seminars. In this dialogue the participant (Melanie) is doing her best to brag, but you can see how difficult it is for her.

MELANIE: People have told me *I'm very resourceful* and I think . . . I guess I'm good at delegating.

INSTRUCTOR: Remove "People have told me," and simply say, "I'm very resourceful."

MELANIE: Oh, that sounds so conceited.

INSTRUCTOR: Try saying it like it's just a matter of fact.

MELANIE: I'm very resourceful. (*flat tone*)

INSTRUCTOR: How did that feel?

MELANIE: Oh, my goodness, that's hard to say. I feel like someone's going to jump up and tell everyone I'm lying.

INSTRUCTOR: Is it true, Melanie? Are you very resourceful?

MELANIE: I'm extremely resourceful. I've figured out ways of doing things at our company that have saved hundreds of thousands of dollars.

INSTRUCTOR: Terrific. Tell us that!

Although bragging can seem too potent to some women, the reality is never "over the top." It is simple, strong, and confident. So, try boasting. It will sound like confidence to everyone else. Promoting yourself in practice sessions—at home, with your friends, and in conversations with yourself—is a great beginning. But the goal, of course, is to bring these skills to those situations where you can position yourself for success in the corporate world.

Promoting Yourself in Every Situation

Self-promotion is not something you can turn on and off. It needs to be a mindset. It becomes part of your identity. You'll want to bring it to all situations in which you communicate. Let's look at some of the situations where self-promotion is a must.

Daily Meetings

Observing men (and women) who flourish at meetings shows the importance of (1) being visible; (2) trumpeting success; (3) sharing excitement; (4) claiming the glory! It doesn't mean you can't give credit to those actually doing the work. But you need to sell *your* accomplishments and link them to broader goals. Deborah, a director of human resources and graduate of Taking the Stage observed, "A couple of weeks after the training, I was asked to present at our leadership retreat. I prepared a PowerPoint on what I wanted to talk about. But this time I added another slide—one that allowed me to brag about the year-to-date accomplishments of HR. I was amazed at how comfortable I was presenting that!"

Every time you put your hand up in a meeting, you have an opportunity to promote yourself. Ju Choon Lian in Malaysia took the initiative in a meeting to discuss how—working with peers and vendors—she helped implement a program that improved the procurement process and brought about cost savings of 10 to 25 percent a year. But the even bigger win was the recognition she received and management's decision to strengthen the procurement process throughout the company.

You don't need a big win to boast. Simply expressing an idea with strength and confidence will enable you to sell yourself as a thought leader with a clear and compelling contribution. You can promote yourself in meetings in many ways: by sharing successful projects, contributing high level thinking, and setting forth compelling ideas.

Performance Reviews

Women need to take the stage here too. One seminar participant observed that there is a "noticeable difference in performance reviews between the way men present themselves and the way women do. Men are a little more apt to say, 'I did this, I did that,' whereas women say, 'The *group* did this, the *group* did that.' Women give credit to others."

The best way to ensure that you promote yourself in your next performance review is to prepare key messages of accomplishment. As one HR manager named Linda told us, "I now list the things I've done when preparing for my performance review; I'm very careful to say 'I led this project' or 'I met my targets,' whereas before I used to give the credit to everyone else. It was always hard for me to say that 'I did something.' So I make a list of my accomplishments during the year to keep it top of mind. I share these successes with my boss during my review, and also during more casual meetings. It is uncomfortable, but I have been able to do it." Kimberly, a director of security and government compliance, agrees: "It was time to complete my midyear review with my manager. I knew what my group had achieved and added my accomplishments in reaching those targets. It was a stretch for me, since I always had difficulty voicing my achievements. But I enunciated my key points, trying not to laugh, which I do when I am nervous. My manager gave me the highest rating possible and superb comments that made me proud. So it was all worth it!"

Career Conversations

Career conversations provide another venue for setting forth your accomplishments—and making a case for the next promotion. No one can or will do it for you. It is assumed that if you don't have the passion to sell yourself, you aren't right for that senior position. Yet when we coach women for their job interviews we hear versions of this as an opener: "I don't know why you'd be seeing me for this position. There are so many others in this organization that could do this job just as well." This woman thinks she is profiling herself as a nice person—not as power mad, ruthless, and greedy. But the interviewer will likely take her at face value and think she lacks self-esteem.

Diane, a vice president in a bank, came to me for coaching because she had "blown it" in a job interview her CEO had lined up for her. Unfortunately, she hadn't felt like she had to sell herself during the interview, because she thought the endorsement of the CEO would be sufficient to land her the job. The result? She got passed up. The top executive doing the hiring told me that she "didn't appear hungry enough. There are at least seven men in line for that job who are far hungrier." When I pressed Diane for her side of the story, I saw the reasons behind her poor performance.

- First, she approached the situation with *ambivalence*. She said that she was not even sure she really *wanted* the job; it would mean going into a different part of the organization, and she liked where she was.

- Second, she *did not prepare* for the interview, because she had come with her CEO's endorsement.
- Third, she *didn't speak with passion*. She came across as passive; she decided that because the interviewer was "low key," she would be, too—so as not to intimidate him.
- Fourth, she *did not deflect criticism*. When the interviewer raised questions about her ability to handle the job, she agreed with him, "just to be polite."

Contrast that negative scenario with the following positive one in which a woman DID sell herself—and got the job. Jennifer was an executive of a major financial corporation. She didn't know where the next big job would come from, but she was determined to move ahead. One day, she was having lunch with the head of HR, who told her she was having difficulty finding someone who could oversee a major international acquisition the firm was undertaking. It would involve integrating the two firms, and spending a significant amount of time in Europe doing so. Jennifer immediately remarked, "What about me?" She proceeded to explain why she felt she had all the qualifications for the position, and shortly after that she got the assignment. It was a major career opportunity for her. In the first example, the woman was virtually handed the job on a silver platter, but lost it; in the second, the woman was not even being considered but got the job because she made a case for herself.

Even if you think you're a shoe-in, you still have to sell yourself. Potential employers and future bosses want you to be strong, confident, and eager. In fact, I advise all my clients to convince themselves they badly want the job before they go to the interview.

Client Meetings

You'll never close a sale—with external or internal clients—unless you promote yourself and your firm to them. You can have the best product in the world, but if you don't show your passion for it, they won't buy it. One thing I have always found critical in selling my firm's services is the single-minded certainty that they cannot find what I am offering anywhere else.

Think of how that outlook can serve you. Every time you go into a customer's office, make a pitch, or propose something to an internal business partner, think, "They need me even more than they can imagine." That is not an arrogant statement; if you have a great product, service, or idea, it is absolutely true. And it will give you inner confidence during that meeting. It will change your voice, body language, messages, and overall presence.

Promoting yourself to clients also requires determination. There is no better example of the persistence required than the following one in which skincare magnate Estée Lauder sought to get her cosmetic line into New York–based Neiman Marcus stores. She met with the store manager and was turned down. As she left the store, she saw company president Stephen Marcus going home, and approached him with these words: "I'm Estée Lauder and I have the most wonderful beauty products in the world and they must be in your store." When Marcus responded that she should be talking to their merchandising manager, she replied, "I have done that, and he said that I should come back another day. But—you see, Mr. Marcus, I don't have time for that because my products must be in your store right away." Her salesmanship proved successful, for he replied, "How much space do you need?" and "When can you have your merchandise here?"[4]

She had brought a big bag filled with merchandise, and the very next day she set it up and she was in business at Neiman Marcus. Stopping everyone who came in the door, she said, "Try this. I'm Estée Lauder and these are the most wonderful beauty products in the world." Marcus later explained, "She was a very determined salesperson . . . and gracious and lovely through it all. It was easier to say yes to Estée than to say no."[5] This is the kind of determination you must show if you want to get ahead.

It can be challenging to promote yourself in this way—at least at the beginning. It involves moving beyond humility, having a clear goal, and using your personal selling skills in every possible situation. But the more you do it, the more comfortable you'll become—and the more natural it will feel. If you are willing to fight for yourself, others are more likely to believe in you and what you are offering them.

Advice for Leaders of Women

Although some women are superb at self-promotion, many others have never developed this ability. You can mentor them in this important skill.

- Encourage women to "toot their own horns" by asking them about wins, awards, accomplishments, or other leadership milestones. Don't just praise women for these things; ask them to *talk about them*.
- Teach them how to promote themselves and their ideas. For example, if someone wants to take on a new project, say, "So tell me why you feel well suited to take on this project."
- Use performance reviews and career discussions to encourage women to sell themselves. Let them know in advance that you want them to put forward their best case for what they have done.
- Make sure those presenting are well rehearsed before a big meeting.

Chapter Seven

Be Courageous

Mary Jane, a human resources specialist in Manila, is a superb example of how to act with courage. As she puts it, "Courage enabled me to take the stage not just in my career but even in my personal life. I used to be very hesitant to express my views or opinions; I got this from growing up in a family where traditional Chinese views are very much present. I remember during my first job, my feet were shaking and I kept on mumbling whenever my boss who was seventy-five years old came to me and asked me questions. I had this fear that if I say 'no' to what he wants us to implement, I will be punished, just like saying 'no' to parents. During Taking the Stage, the discussion showed me that hey, we need to speak for ourselves, express our opinions and views. The discussion about saying NO really got my attention, and gave me the courage to say 'no' and realize it's not a disrespectful way of expressing your views."

Courage is important for women, because there are so many situations in which we have to break through barriers, challenge traditional behaviors, and redefine the way others see us. Indeed, if you're a woman in the corporate world, you often have to show more courage than a man would. Courage becomes your secret weapon. But boldness, by itself, is not what I'm advocating. Indeed, on its own it can be foolhardy. What's needed is courage that is undertaken with *intelligence* and *good judgment*. Here are examples of key areas where we must demonstrate bravery.

Courage to Put Your Hand Up

The most basic expression of courage is putting your hand up to speak. Mirjam in the Netherlands said she "took the stage by volunteering to give a presentation in our [Taking the Stage] seminar." She explained, "It was a big step for me, because most of the time before that I would have just waited until somebody else volunteered. But it felt really good afterward and it wasn't as scary as I thought." Following the seminar, "we as a department had to give a presentation, so without hesitation I told my manager that I wanted to do it. I knew, once again, that I could have kept my mouth shut, but I really wanted to present. My colleagues joked that I could do it another time, and I said, 'No way!'" The lesson we all can take away from this story is that the more you put your hand up to speak, the easier and more fun it gets.

The bravery needed to speak up can be all the greater when a woman finds herself as the single female among men. She is often afraid that the men in the room will interrupt, ignore, tease, or challenge her. As one woman, a director of information security, told us, "Our weekly manage-ment meetings have always been a source of anxiety for me. When sitting around the table with assertive, ambitious men, I chose to observe and listen rather than compete for air time." Yet, not speaking up is a tacit admission that the men control the conversation and have the power. Every woman who remains silent is contributing to that reality. You will be respected far more—for your thoughts and your courage—than you would if you were to remain silent.

If you can find the courage to speak up at least once in every meeting you attend, you'll be on your way. The more often you do it, the easier it will become.

Courage to Challenge Others

Courage is also required when you challenge other people's views. Some-times we live with an uncomfortable reality: we don't want to disagree with other people, particularly not authority figures. But we want to bring our concerns to their attention if we believe we are in the right. And we must do so with firmness, respect, and a script that emphasizes a reasoned argument. This is a familiar challenge for women—one that's evident in the following story told by someone who had the courage to speak her mind to her boss.

As she explained, "I had been stressed out for the past six months because my boss had been challenging me on some things she thought I should be doing differently. So finally I was able to say 'I disagree with you. I've done this, and this, and this.' Previously I might have said to myself, 'Okay I'll go away and take that.' But this time I finally said to myself, 'I'M NOT TAKING IT ANYMORE.'" The speaker was right to raise this important issue if she felt undermined, but it's best to adopt a collaborative approach rather than venting and using confrontational language like "I disagree." Acknowledge the other person's point of view and then introduce yours by saying, "I see the situation somewhat differently." Don't let your anger build up to the point where you become confrontational.

A great example of having the courage to challenge others comes from a junior employee in a high-tech firm who had just completed a company-wide diversity program. At an all-employee event she realized that the CEO and his leadership team who sat together on the stage were all white males. She thought, "This picture doesn't make sense." So during the Q&A period she asked the CEO, "Why has the company put all employees through diversity training and yet the management team are all white males? Are you saying that diversity doesn't mean anything? Or is the situation about to change?" She was trembling so much that she didn't even hear his reply. When the session was over, her male colleagues said, "Wow, how could you ever do something like that? Start packing your bags!" The women said, "Go girl!"

A few weeks later the CEO called her into his office, and although she was afraid he was going to fire her, she found, instead, that her act of daring paid off! He offered her a job. He said he wanted someone with her boldness to work for him. She became his executive assistant, and from there her career took off—and she eventually became head of a large sales organization. Why had her courage to challenge him been so well received? She addressed an important issue that her audience—the CEO—*had* to take seriously. And he did take it seriously, because she spoke politely, positively, dispassionately, and without personally embarrassing him. She was handsomely rewarded for being so smartly courageous.

Courage to Take On a New Role

It often takes courage to pursue the next leadership opportunity or promotion, and that bravery is crucial for anyone who wants to move from the wings to center stage.

Karen Strauss Cook, who became the first woman hired in Goldman Sachs's Equities Division and the firm's first trader, was a floor clerk in the New York Stock Exchange when she marched into Goldman Sachs—résumé in hand—foregoing the usual route of applying in writing and hoping they'd reply. She asked the receptionist if there was someone she could talk to about being hired. The receptionist wouldn't give her a name, and the two were in a standoff for some time, until, according to Cook, "I noticed someone pacing back and forth in the hallway just behind us. He finally stops, turns to me, and asks, 'Who are you and what is it that you want?'" It was Robert Rubin (who later became US Treasury Secretary). When it was clear she was not going away, he interviewed her on the spot—and eleven interviews later, she was hired into a brilliant career.[1] Cook exemplified the determination and moxie women need to break into more senior positions.

Courage at times means taking risks, for example, in assuming a new role or responsibilities. Richard Nesbitt, CEO of CIBC World Markets, advises, "Most people take too little risk in their personal careers. People, both men and women, should be prepared to take on a new job that is outside their comfort zone, or one that is in a different country, or even a role that might involve a pay cut in the short run that will help them achieve a promotion in the long run. This offers the opportunity to demonstrate the ability to succeed in a different set of circumstances, or if they don't succeed, it also offers them the opportunity to show how they deal with failure. No one has unbridled success for thirty years. When I hire a senior executive, I always look for when they failed and how they dealt with it." So risk taking can even involve the courage to fail—and the willingness to grow from that experience.

Courage to assume a new role can also mean breaking free completely and moving on to a totally new career path. I took such a bold step when I left a corporate job to start my own company. There were so many naysayers. Some of my best friends told me, "You're crazy!" But this story has a happy ending because I did create a firm—and we've enjoyed great success.

Courage to Break Into the Boys' Club

Breaking into the "boys' club" (or any clique) takes courage. And in many organizations there definitely is a boys' club. Women know that—and so do the men.

One senior banker, Melissa, who works in the trading room of a major financial institution, said, "The trading floor is a dog-eat-dog world. I was devastated when I came here from investment banking and I told my mentor, 'I can't work here, I want my old job back.' It made me uncomfortable that people on the trading floor were swearing, carrying on, and yelling at each other. Men are very different from women. They talk to you like you don't exist and they don't listen to you when you're speaking to them. I said to the recruiter, 'I want out. This is not the environment for me.'" It was a corporate version of the locker room.

But Melissa had an answer: developing inner strength. As she explained, "My mentor sat me down and said, 'You have the personality and drive to be in this job. You have to grow some thick skin and pull yourself away from everyone else.' And I did. It took guts, but I basically set the rules for everyone on the desk. I said, 'I'm here for business. I'm not here for pleasure. And we're here to make money. So let's all work together as a group.' I think when women set those ground rules guys know 'I can't mess with Melissa.' They labeled me The Ball Buster; but at least they realized they couldn't walk all over me."

Rather than calling the men out on each sexist comment, Melissa shared a vision of how things should work. As for the Ball Buster title, the goal in breaking through the boys' club is not necessarily being liked or being one of the boys. It involves being respected, working side by side in a collegial fashion. And if we get labeled for being strong, so be it. The more enlightened men—and there are more and more of them—will come around and appreciate such strength.

Courage to Be Yourself

Women must develop the courage to be themselves. "If you're a woman in the corporate world," says former Pfizer EVP and general counsel Amy Schulman, "you tend to view interactions as a litmus test for whether you belong."[2] We give too much power to the signals—a smile, a frown, a blink of the eye, a stare, a critical comment.

In the face of such pressures and judgments from our colleagues, we shouldn't lose those wonderful qualities that make us individuals. Don't let others—those in power, or those in "the club"—isolate you or make you feel judged or unworthy. Don't let them deprive you of your spontaneity, your energy, your vitality, your sense of humor, your ideas. Don't "play to" your audience. Women often give their audience smiles if they want smiles or speak with perky voices if they feel their audience wants "niceness." Women are good actors—and we can be nice, cutesy, perky, flirty, or anything else if we feel others want us to be that way. But if you do that, your very essence will dissolve and nothing will be left of you.

Do this: give some thought to the qualities you value in yourself—such as warmth, passion, empathy, clear thinking, and conviction. Make sure you express these qualities whenever you speak. Let them together form your "authentic self." Arm yourself with them whenever you feel judged, attacked, or ignored. They will give you the strength to be yourself. And express them consistently in every encounter, rather than mimicking the style and attributes of those you're talking to.

Courage takes many forms: putting your hand up, challenging others, taking on a new role to advance your career, dealing with men, or remaining true to yourself. Courage will get you through these situations, and power you forward on your path to success.

Advice for Leaders of Women

Courage is an Achilles' heel for many women. There are so many situations that require their bravery—from speaking up at a meeting, to taking on a new role, to dealing with an environment where they may feel isolated, to being comfortable with who they are. Here are the ways you can encourage courage.

- Prompt those who are less outspoken to contribute to a meeting by saying something like, "I'd like to hear Marissa's view on that—she has been very close to the project."
- If someone loses her courage while defending her view, ask her to continue.
- Talk to women about taking on new roles or assignments, and bolster their confidence if you think they are fearful, reluctant, or undecided.
- Help them find ways to deal with feelings that they aren't part of "the boys' club" and the daily pressures that creates.
- Push them out of their comfort zone and support them when they fail.

Chapter Eight

Hold Your Ground

I once received a phone call from a university I attended, letting me know I had won a three-year graduate fellowship. After thanking them I asked, "How much is the stipend?" The head of admissions said, "$2,500 a year plus tuition." (This was a LONG time ago!) I paused, realizing that it would be difficult to live on that amount, and replied, "Is everyone offered that same amount?" "Just the women," was the response. "The men get more because their fathers aren't taking care of them." That seemed unfair to me. So I responded, "Well, my father doesn't take care of me, and I need the same as the men." And that's what I got.

Despite the fact that this happened many years ago, that story's lesson is still true: we women need to advocate for ourselves and hold our ground when it comes to standing firmly for what we believe is rightfully ours. I could have accepted the initial offer and taken out more student loans (which I already had in abundance); but I pushed back to get what I felt I deserved. It wasn't bravery that led me to fire back. It was the principle of it. Many times women give way too easily. We end up with less than we deserve. If you want to lead, you must *hold your ground*.

Women are so concerned to be agreeable and supportive that they tend to give in too easily. When someone contradicts, interrupts, or undercuts a woman, she often backs down or, even worse, *apologizes* to make the other individual feel better. Then she ends up feeling badly and gives the impression that she is not confident or strong.

Holding your ground does not mean becoming belligerent, refusing to listen, or rushing to strike back. It means standing up for yourself and your ideas when necessary. Make your case based on substance and facts—not emotions. The following situations show the importance of standing firm if you want to keep your place on stage.

If Someone Interrupts You

Women frequently are interrupted, and a study entitled "Against Our Will: Male Interruptions of Females in Cross-Sex Conversations,"[1] found that men initiated 75 percent of all gender-based interruptions. According to Barbara Annis and John Gray in their book, *Work with Me*, men also interrupt each other and will "cut into a conversation to toss in their opinion or build on someone else's contribution with a better idea. It's a lot like passing a ball back and forth as players move down field to score a point."[2] This "male" style of communicating can be "unnatural and unmannerly to women."[3] Many women simply stop speaking, and feel frustrated that they haven't been able to get their ideas across. That response will not allow you to complete your thought or gain you respect.

Annis and Gray, who see women's style of communicating as more exploratory than men's, encourage women to begin their conversations with a clear setup—for example, "I would like your opinion about something, but let me first give you [the] background." This lets the men in the room know there will be time for their views.

If you are still interrupted as you are speaking, there are various approaches you can take. You might simply keep talking with firmness. That works for many people, and the person who broke in has no choice but to wait for you to finish. You might also say, "I'd like to finish" or "There's another point I was making." Or simply but politely say, "Hold on!" And to give yourself still greater visual impact, raise your hand, palm open indicating you are not ready for their interruption. But don't *ask* permission to continue, as in "Can I please finish?" because it's not a favor you're requesting. Look the interrupter in the eye and hold your gaze until you have reclaimed your side of the conversation.

What about interruptions when you are giving a presentation? Even though these may be well intentioned, don't feel you have to address them as they come up. Some speakers invite questions. But too many remarks from the audience can slow you down, distract from the flow of your ideas, and potentially create opposition—or at the very least, prompt a discussion before you have made your case. A seasoned facilitator in a logistics firm told me she was continually being interrupted by questions. "So, now," she said, "I tell the group to save their questions until the end of the session. It has helped bolster my confidence and keep me on track." If you're going to take that approach, explain this at the outset.

If Someone Takes Your Idea

How often do women think, "Hey, that was my idea . . . Why are people hearing it from him and not from me?" This "idea theft" can occur for a variety of reasons. It may reflect the "male" desire to solve a problem. It is also possible that you weren't clear enough or convincing enough for people to really hear you. Your approach to the topic may have been exploratory, while the men in the room wanted closure. If so, let the other person continue, because attacking the offender will sound feeble and self-serving.

But if you feel you have spoken clearly and the other person is deliberately echoing your idea, step in and claim it as your own. Humor can be useful in such situations. One woman at a global technology firm found that her colleague kept repeating her ideas. She finally said, "Didn't I just say that? . . . Is there an echo in here?" Or you might remark to the offender, "I'm glad you agree with me, Bob," or "That makes two of us now who are arguing for that strategy. I'd like to know who here supports our recommendation." You not only show you have authored the idea; you now take the lead away from Bob and seek support from the room.

If Someone Challenges You

When someone challenges you, respond with facts, not feelings. If you respond emotionally, you will sound weak. Many women *take criticism personally* by becoming angry or defensive. The following example shows the HR director responding defensively:

MALE EXECUTIVE: We don't need to hire a new leasing manager.
FEMALE HR DIRECTOR: I don't know why you're questioning me. That's my decision to make. It's an HR call.

Responding in this manner weakens the HR director's position and convinces no one. It's far better to present a substantive case for your recommendation, as in the following:

MALE EXECUTIVE: We don't need to hire a new leasing manager.
FEMALE HR DIRECTOR: I understand you're committed to keeping costs down, but I have had discussions with the leasing managers, and they're feeling over-whelmed and can't handle all the opportunities out there in the market. By adding one more to the team, we'll be better positioned to build market share.

It's easy to fall into the emotional trap when you are challenged. Even Margaret Thatcher earlier in her career turned aggressive when she felt criticized. She said, referring to herself, "This animal, if attacked, defends itself, so when I come up against somebody who is obviously out to do a very belligerent interview, I say to myself, 'By God, anything you can do I can do better,' and I'm belligerent back!"[4] This feisty approach didn't work for her, and she was coached by her advisor, Gordon Reece, to be more empathetic. She did in fact soften her style.[5]

If someone challenges you because they want to see if you're prepared or confident in what you're saying, respond by showing them you *are* confident. The best response is to be at the top of your game. One female managing director told me, "Men sometimes pick holes in what you're saying. They're thinking, 'She's a woman and she doesn't know what she is doing. She is a weaker link in our world.' So they zing you with a question they'd never zing another man with. They might challenge your numbers. I am very much aware when this occurs, and I make sure I know my stuff inside and out—because I know some guy is going to say, 'That doesn't make sense. Are you sure that's right?' And I'll be able to say, 'Yeah, actually it is and here is the background.' The last thing you want is to be caught off guard by some question when you are in a meeting with twenty men."

When someone challenges you, listen carefully to what they say. Not every question is hostile or designed to trip you up. Sometimes good questions will help you sharpen your thinking. You might begin with an acknowledgment of the person's position: "I can understand why you ask that question" or "That is a question we often get." Then present your thinking as clearly and succinctly as you can. If you are certain of your facts, hold your ground and explain your position. State, "I stand behind that number because . . ." or "That number was arrived at by . . ." But in other cases, you can respond, "I can certainly look into what you suggest and get back to you."

Come back with confidence as well when someone challenges your ability to deliver. One young sales professional was at a meeting and she hadn't come close to reaching her sales targets for the year. So her boss said, "Are you going to miss your numbers?" Without skipping a beat she said, "I'm going to make them." She didn't tell him how, but she went to every single one of her major customers and told them that she absolutely needed to close sales. And they were so moved that they gave her the business she needed to meet her targets.

In all these situations, respond dispassionately and make your best case. When challenged, present your strongest arguments, not your strongest emotions. To keep from getting emotional, understand that challenges are not necessarily hostile. Women's rituals of interaction are different from male rituals. A female client said, "I just don't get it. We're in a meeting and the men are challenging each other and me in a very aggressive way. The men leave the room laughing and making plans for golf and I'm seething for two weeks. How can they do that?" They can because it is ritualistic behavior for the men. It is *not* an expression of hostility. It is important that we become aware of the ritualistic nature of this behavior so we can keep from feeling that challenges are hostile.

If Someone Blindsides You

Despite your best efforts to get buy-in for your ideas, people—and that includes even those you thought were your allies—can surprise you with their sharp criticism. But don't let them unnerve you.

In a global conference call with one of the world's biggest technology companies, a woman spoke of a meeting with high-level executives in which she became unsettled. She had done all the prep work behind the scenes to make sure everybody was comfortable with her presentation and had gotten prior agreement from all parties. But she was blindsided during the presentation by one senior individual who now sharply criticized the plan. The woman became visibly upset and her eyes began to tear up. She told herself, "I can't cry in this meeting," but she didn't know what her comeback strategy should be.

The answer is to *depersonalize* the situation. If you act out of emotion, and show anger and hurt at what you perceive as a betrayal, you'll only weaken your cause. Instead, take yourself out of the equation and come back with a confident but composed case for your project or idea. Even if you've made the arguments before, make them again. And begin with generosity to bring opposing viewpoints on your side: "I understand your position." Or, "I'm pleased to respond to your concern." Take the high ground, and view every challenge as an opportunity to influence.

If you're blindsided in a one-on-one conversation with a boss or colleague, adopt the same strategy: rise above your feelings and focus on substance. A young woman in HR told me about such an exchange with her boss. She asked him at the end of a one-on-one meeting to give her feedback on her performance. Because they'd had a good meeting, she expected a positive response. Instead the boss began, "You asked for feedback. Let me sum it up this way: I want meat and potatoes from you. You are lettuce and tomatoes." She was in shock and opted for silence in the face of this odd culinary critique. But the best course of action would have been not to take those comments personally, but to come back with strength. She might have said, "Can you be more specific?" Asking him to explain would have shown that she was strong enough to hear the truth.

If Someone Is Sexist toward You

Sexist comments deserve pushback from us—and a clear statement that they are out of bounds. I've encountered discriminatory policies and sexist comments more than once in my career. The first day of my corporate life

I was waiting in reception for my boss or his assistant when a male manager came out, looked me over and said, "Are you the temp I ordered?" I felt like I was his take-out order. That was my first, but hardly my last encounter with sexism. A particularly sharp exchange came when I was a younger member of a PR department at a financial institution. I was in a meeting with my boss, a vice president, and other members of our team. We were discussing the layout for an employee publication. We came to page 4, and my boss said, "Judith, you can be our Sunshine Girl," referring to a feature on page 4 of the *Toronto Sun* showing a bikini-clad woman. My response to him: "That's an unprofessional remark." It didn't help my relationship with him, but that's okay because we usually outlast people who have that mentality. In fact, I went on to establish my own company shortly after that, and he faded from sight.

The important thing is to keep your focus and not let such comments rattle you or change the agenda. A young engineer in a technology firm went to her boss to explain her thinking on the topic being discussed, and something she said must have unnerved him, because he stopped her and said, "You know what you are? You're a bold, brassy bitch." She looked at him and without flinching replied, "Well, at least you've heard me." Unsurprisingly, this young engineer, who showed extraordinary focus under the circumstance, eventually became a senior executive, one of the top five women in a global company.

Many firms are becoming more enlightened. Standing up to sexism increasingly is not only the right thing to do personally; it also gains you respect from both men and women in the organization. To that end, women must be very careful not to position themselves as sexual objects. Maria Bartiromo, who for two decades covered the New York Stock Exchange for CNBC's *Closing Bell*, and today does the same for Fox News, is often referred to as "The Money Honey." In 2007 she applied to trademark the "Money Honey" name across a host of consumer products. But she has given up those marks, saying, "I probably will not be using the Money Honey name."[6] That's a great decision. Could you imagine a serious male reporter being labeled the "Stock Jock"? Although branding herself this way may make her more appealing, it reinforces a stereotype and doesn't help women who are fighting sexism in the workplace. It also gives men mixed signals. I have worked with so many male leaders as clients, and I believe the vast majority want to do the right thing by women. So women need to provide clear direction. That means not relating as a sex object, not flirting, not taking it as a compliment if someone finds you attractive and "hustles" you.

If Someone Bullies You

A chapter about holding your ground wouldn't be complete without a discussion of bullying. This has traditionally been a source of anxiety for many women and can lead to the departure of strong, capable women that organizations need. The problem is, it is often unknown and goes unacknowledged. Women don't always want to report it; many consider it embarrassing to them or fear they'll be labeled as troublemakers if they do.

I once coached a talented, organized HR director who was by all accounts a star performer. But her boss was a bully who would toy with her. He once jokingly replied when she asked about the succession planning process, "You are in the succession plan, but we don't know what to do with you. You have no future in this company. You'll have to go elsewhere. Maybe you can find a job at the lumberyard down the street." What should she have done? Well, it's a tough situation. I would normally say, "Reply dispassionately"—but the hostility in the boss's comment made it nearly impossible to do so. She responded with anger and he replied, "I like to see you riled up. That way I know I can get my way." She could also have accepted that it might be the wrong time to discuss this subject with her boss, and set up a meeting at another time to do so. If situations like this persist, one solution is to report it to HR. The other is to leave. And that is exactly what she did, and she has never looked back. Another firm is now benefiting from her talent. If you feel your corporate setting is not appreciating the qualities you value in yourself, it just might be time to find another place where you will be valued.

The best way to respond when others challenge our views is with reason and substance—not by getting emotional. When we personalize a situation, we overreact and give our audience too much power to judge us. Such (imagined) judgments can silence us—so refuse to accept them. Instead, dispassionately deliver the arguments that show you are unfazed by what was said and that you stand firmly on higher ground.

This chapter has discussed difficult situations that may arise in the workplace and require you to hold your ground. It's important to emphasize that despite the male/female nature of these examples, *many male leaders are on your side.* They do not want to see (or have you experience) bullying, sexism, or intimidation of any kind. I learned that lesson many years ago when I was coaching a client—a COO of a well-known aircraft company—and I found myself in a situation where I had to politely but firmly reject his advances. Later I learned from the CEO that my client had been fired. I confided, "I'm glad he's gone, because he was quite forward with me." The CEO replied, "I wish you had told me that. It would have given me still another reason to fire him." At that moment I learned an important lesson: men can be our champions and advocates in such situations. This is even truer today, as leaders increasingly seek to create inclusive, respectful organizations. So hold your ground, but realize that you are not alone. Don't feel you have to bury these problems. Stand on firm footing with those who support you and value you—men and women alike.

Advice for Leaders of Women

Women can feel intimidated by a variety of situations—from being interrupted to being treated as a sexual object to being bullied. When you create a healthy workplace environment, you strengthen your organization as a whole and broaden the opportunities for women. To this end:

- Eliminate from the work environment anything that represents intimidation, harassment, interruptions, stealing (ideas), bullying, or sexism.
- When someone is interrupted in meetings, say, "I don't believe Maria was finished." For bullying or sexism, say, "Let's be respectful"; and if

someone is stealing ideas, you may interject, "I believe you are agreeing with what Isabelle said."

- In addition to publicly intervening, speak to the offending individual privately to explain that this is inappropriate behavior.
- Let it be known through emails or the coaching you give to your team that you expect a culture of mutual respect and inclusiveness, and tell them what this means.

Part Two

Create a Strong Script

Chapter Nine

Portray Yourself as a Leader

T he Humphrey Group works with many female leaders around the world, and the scripts they have created for themselves do not always project confident leadership. Some tell us they wish they could present their arguments more convincingly in meetings—they have great ideas but can't always get them across with strength or clarity. Others tell us they're good at setting forth their views in small groups, but they would like to be more effective at inspiring the room when they give major presentations. Still others say that when it comes to job interviews, they would like to be better at selling themselves. And almost all the women we deal with would like to sound more confident and convincing in everyday conversations such as phone and conference calls, hallway chats, and elevator conversations.

To take the stage and have others see you as a dynamic leader requires that you create strong scripts for all these occasions. When I say "scripts," I don't simply mean the texts for formal speeches and presentations. This term refers more broadly to the words we use for *every* encounter—from town halls to phone calls, from elevator chats to client encounters.

Part 2 of this book shows you how to create those powerful scripts. The starting point is to ask, "How do I want to portray myself?" Creating a positive profile of yourself is at the heart of a strong script.

We Focus on Our Flaws, Fears, and Foibles

Men tend to take pride in their strengths, and accept compliments, whereas women are more likely to point out their flaws, disclose their fears, and dismiss their strengths. Let's look at some of the ways we do this in our scripts.

We Share Our Insecurities

Whether we are new to the business world or seasoned executives, women share their insecurities. It's that inner crow talking! Some time ago, I arrived just as a female CEO was about to speak to a packed crowd at a women's luncheon. She stepped up to the podium and confessed to the audience, "I don't like public speaking." The crowd grew hushed, but unfortunately she didn't stop there. "I've tried to drill down and figure out why I so dislike public speaking," she said, "and I've concluded that it's because I feel alone when I speak publicly. . . . I feel without a connection to the people in the room." She meandered on for forty minutes, and when she finally came to the end of her remarks she shared more of her insecurities: "That's my story. I don't have any words of wisdom I can dispel. I don't know if I've been helpful." This highly successful head of her own company—a global technology firm— saw herself in such negative terms that she shocked her audience. And chances are, they ended up seeing her that way as well.

It's not just our major speeches and presentations that betray our insecurities. We convey these in passing comments, too. A woman might say, "I'm not sure I've pulled together all the information we need for this meeting" or "I don't know if all of you on the conference call can hear me. . . . Is my voice too soft?" or "That was a silly thing for me to say." Such comments can undermine people's confidence in us— and it's important to be aware of this. As one woman said, "I used to joke and make light of myself, saying things like 'I can't get this spreadsheet to open up' but I realized I need to quit making fun of myself if I want people to take me seriously."

We Call Attention to Our Physical Flaws

Why do we accentuate what we *feel* are flaws (and what other people likely don't even notice)? I once was introduced by a woman who came to the mic and told the large audience that she hadn't known when she got up that morning that she would be introducing me, and unfortunately she had put on a poorly fitting suit and an ugly belt. It was an inauspicious opening. I recall feeling sorry for her and thinking that her negative self-portrayal was so unnecessary. On another occasion, I heard a senior executive walk up to the podium and after looking at her audience say, "Is my hair alright? It looked really weird to me this morning." Can you imagine a man talking about his poorly fitting pinstripes or his bad haircut?

We Shun Our Success

We women also downplay our success. I attended a meeting with several top women in a corporation. As they introduced themselves, nearly every one apologized for the fact that she had made it to the top. One said, "I cannot believe I'm a senior vice president." Another remarked, "I don't know how I got to this level." And a third confided, "My title may sound impressive, but my job isn't!" Words like these cast us in minor parts, even when others have given us leading roles. I once asked a new client what her title was and she replied, "VP, but I feel like I'm old to be where I am today." Instead of being proud, she felt like an "over-the-hill" VP.

Hiding our achievements is detrimental to our careers. One director I know never told her peers when she'd achieved major goals. She thought it would be a waste of everyone's time. But her colleagues drew the conclusion that she never completed these strategic undertakings, and they gave her poor scores on peer evaluations. She's now looking for a job.

We Deflect Compliments

Try praising a woman for a stylish watch or an outfit she's wearing, and she well may say, "I got this on sale" or "It looks expensive but it's not." If you thank a woman for a presentation well done, you're likely to hear, "Really? I was so nervous." If you tell a woman you like her necklace, she'll reply, "I love your gorgeous shoes"—as a way of showing she's no better than you. I once complimented a female VP of HR on a lovely small purse she was carrying, and she said, "I had to buy this because I had a bruised shoulder. Believe it or not, the filing drawer in my office cabinet flew out and hit me and I was on the floor, under my desk in pain. I went to therapy, and everyone else had these glamorous injuries, gotten on the ski slopes. But my injury? Hit by a filing cabinet drawer." My mental picture of this woman will always be of her lying on the floor by her desk bruised, rather than carrying a beautiful purse.

We Play the Wrong "Characters"

Women also sometimes miscast themselves at work by acting flirtatious with colleagues or maternal in the board room. One of our instructors taught a seminar with scientists who were mapping the human genome. There was one woman in the group—and she was a powerhouse. Presence, poise. A keen intelligence. Within thirty minutes of the start of the session, she had been reduced to a giggling teenager by one of the male participants. He undermined her presentation with gentle gibes that she found amusing. His charm essentially dismantled her authority. It wasn't something either one was doing consciously; but she allowed him to weaken her role nonetheless. She went from "leader in the scientific community" to "cute girl." Some of us easily fall into the maternal role, too. A vice president told me, "When I attend the board meetings as the only female executive, it is hard to get a cup of coffee and not ask my male peers if I can get them a cup too. But I have to resist the temptation to play that traditional female role—because I want my colleagues on the board to view me as a peer."

We See Ourselves as Worker Bees

Women also can undercut their leadership when they define themselves as their organization's "worker bees." Their recorded voice mails frequently say, "Sorry, I'm away from my desk." Why should they be tethered to their desks? They also tend to be flattered when their boss says they are "good workers." One female vice president told me, "I took it as a compliment when my boss introduced me [by saying], 'She can handle whatever work we give her, and we are just waiting to see what breaks.'" That really tells a lot about how women as workers are viewed—push her until she breaks! That's hardly the praise bestowed on a leader. Indeed, a Catalyst study entitled "Unwritten Rules: What You Don't Know Can Hurt Your Career"[1] ranked "working long hours" or "energetic, works a lot" very low (29 percent and 31 percent respectively) on the scale of what's important to advancement. In contrast, networking scored high: 71 percent.

Even famous, highly successful women take comfort in describing themselves as "good workers." When Hillary Clinton first arrived on Capitol Hill, she waved off photographers, saying, "I'm a workhorse, not a show horse."[2] In an interview with *Vanity Fair*, actress Sarah Jessica Parker said, "I work and work and work until I can no longer and someone has to remove me from the premises."[3] Did Parker make her millions by working overtime? Not likely. And when asked what made her successful during a talk at Stanford, Yahoo CEO Marissa Mayer responded, "I like to work."[4]

Of course, dedication and drive are important. But it's a myth that simply doing the perfect job will gain us the success we want. How many times have women put in the long hours to produce information-heavy presentations, only to have some man in the room take that information, form it into an idea, and receive praise for his insights. It's important to get past the mounds of information in your day-to-day life. Don't talk about "the work" or take your audience through processes—"We did this, now we are doing this, and by next week we will be doing this." Never use the word *busy*, as in "How are you?" "I've been busy," or "overloaded," or "stressed"—even in a casual elevator conversation.

I'd like to think that women are beginning to realize that coming across as workers does not lead to success. A participant in one of our courses had an *aha* moment when her mentor said, "If you continue to stay at your desk, keeping your head down and working, rather than taking opportunities to meet people or attend meetings or network, you will always be that person at your desk—the workhorse rather than a decision maker and leader at meetings." She explained, "That made me determined to move beyond my office, network and market myself, and build relationships that will allow me to lead."

Come out from the wings and onto the stage where leaders preside. Throw away the scripts that diminish you. Rewrite your scripts!

Create Your Leadership Profile

How can you rewrite your scripts to portray yourself as a confident leader? To begin with, stay on message about your leadership and never undercut yourself. Don't give voice to your insecurities, call attention to physical flaws, ignore your success, deflect compliments, or slip into worker roles or traditional feminine identities. Instead, find a new narrative that *creates a positive identity* for yourself—a leadership "brand." This is the self-image you build in other people's minds when you speak.

You'll find that using the vocabulary of a leader will put you in a much stronger light. Make a list of the top ten words that describe you as the leader you'd like to be, and use them often. It's likely that *inspirational* will be on your list, so tell others, "I am inspired by our vision of what we can accomplish." Inspiration is contagious; if you are inspired, others will be too. You might also use words like *focused, energized,* and *confident* to describe yourself. In a meeting, for example, you might say, "I am *focused* on results" or "I am *energized* by our strategic vision." Dilma Rousseff, president of Brazil, was the first female in the history of the United Nations to open the General Assembly. She spoke eloquently, sharing her values as a female leader: "It is with personal humility, but with my justified pride as a woman that I meet this historic moment." She continued, "Two other words that are very special to me are . . . courage and sincerity. And it is with courage and sincerity that I wish to speak to you today."[5] If you create for yourself a "leader's lexicon"—a list of words that describe you as a leader—and keep using the words on the list, others will come to identify you as a leader with those qualities. And you, too, will see yourself from that perspective and will be motivated to act accordingly.

Leaders are "big picture" thinkers, too, so cultivate your identity as a visionary and strategic thinker. IBM's first female CEO, Virginia Rometty, is a master of vision—something she spoke about in her first speech to shareholders: "We are an innovation company. This means that we pursue continuous transformation. That is why IBM has been in existence for more than 100 years and why we will thrive for another century."[6] Similarly, Marissa Mayer told the press about her plans for growing in a difficult market: "This is a very competitive and a tough space. I don't think that success is by any means guaranteed. My focus is always end-users, great technology and terrific talent."[7] Even though you may not be the head of a global powerhouse like IBM or Yahoo, you must have a vision if you want to be seen as a leader. Big picture thinking requires that you communicate your organization's larger goals.

Thinking expansively also means focusing on and bringing about *solutions*—and that doesn't mean you have to be a senior officer. You can be an HR professional or a business analyst who works effectively with internal clients because you understand *their* goals. Or you may be a member of a cross-functional team and your broad outlook enables you to help build a shared solution. Being a big picture thinker means going beyond your own terrain and getting inside others' minds to help build collaborative solutions.

Keep larger goals in mind wherever you are—in an elevator or speaking at a meeting. If someone at work says, "How's it going?" respond, "We're putting the finishing touches on the strategy" or "That investment is paying off." Portray yourself as a *contributor of ideas*. We are being paid not just for our knowledge, but also to translate that knowledge into ideas that will make a difference. So in meetings don't be afraid to voice your thinking—to raise your hand and say, "As I see it . . ." Or, "Another angle we might consider . . ." Or, "Here's an idea."

Management wants your insights. One female client told me with some surprise that after an executive meeting she'd been to, the CFO said to her, "That was a very astute comment you made in the meeting." At first she couldn't remember what she had said—so oblivious was she to the value she had added to the discussion. When she did realize it, she thought to herself, "I don't put myself on the line enough." You need to be aware of how powerful your ideas can be and express them often and with confidence, so that other people are aware of them too. It's not just the C-level people who need to do so; we all must.

A final point about portraying yourself: have an "elevator story" about yourself ready for any spontaneous situation. When a company goes public with an initial public offering (IPO), its media reps always have a narrative that highlights the company's success and potential for rapid growth. I like to think that we as individuals should have our own IPO stories—call them our Incredible Person Offerings. For example, let's say you're a manager in a software lab. Your story might be as follows: "Hello. I am Sarah Ross—lead manager in Trillium's software lab here in Canada. Last year we developed and launched a new generation of software for HR systems. It's been an exceptionally successful product, adopted across North America and in Europe. I'm proud of what my entire team has accomplished." It's a short but powerful story—and you don't necessarily always tell it in sequence like that. But you would let the details of it come out. As an exercise, write up a one paragraph IPO story on yourself.

In sum, cast yourself as a leader in every situation. Don't put yourself down. Find ways to illuminate your success, and use new narratives that showcase your leadership. Bring them forward in meetings and other situations. You portray your leadership by what you *say*. So the first step in designing your leader's script is to create a strong persona for yourself.

Advice for Leaders of Women

Women often focus on their weaknesses rather than their strengths. As a senior leader, you are in a privileged position to help those on your team see themselves in their best light.

- Encourage women to speak positively about themselves.
- Be careful how you describe women. Saying, "Oh, Susan, she's a hard worker" typecasts a woman as a "doer" rather than a leader. Do you do this more with women than with men?
- Develop a strategy for dealing with people's expressions of insecurity. For example, when a woman dismisses a compliment or rejects praise for a job well done, you might ask her why she does not

believe what she was told. Understanding what she is feeling is important for both of you.

- When a woman demonstrates leadership behaviors, point them out as you would with any of your team. She may not even realize she has those qualities.
- Help women become "big picture" thinkers by complimenting them when they bring forward clear and valuable ideas.

Chapter Ten

Strengthen Your Language

W hen I meet women who have come to our firm for coaching, one of the questions I typically ask is, "How do you feel about your ability to project confidence?" I still remember one woman named Sarah who replied enthusiastically that she now sounds so much more confident than she once did.

As she put it, "A few years back I was perhaps that very apologetic, very cautious female who was always trying to lighten things rather than sounding sure of myself. Recently I have definitely tried to be more forthright, and I think I am sounding more confident, though I am not sure." I was pleased she felt she had progressed so much, but as you can see from her response, her language still showed considerable tentativeness. Words like *perhaps, trying, tried, very, think*, and *not sure* weaken her statements.

Many women are not even aware that the words they choose can sound weak to others. While we often use this self-effacing language to create a more collegial or collaborative atmosphere, it actually diminishes us and ends up making us sound less like leaders. When Margaret Thatcher became leader of the Conservative Party in England in 1975, she spoke as someone who was not comfortable with her leadership role. When a BBC interviewer asked her how she felt about her new responsibilities, she replied, "I've been *so busy* that I *haven't had really much time to think* about it. After all, I know I am still *only me*, and so do my family. But I am very much aware of the responsibilities. And a *little bit apprehensive*. Who wouldn't be, when you *think of the names that I follow?*" [italics mine].[1] Who would believe that was the Iron Lady speaking?

Thatcher eventually became a strong voice with every word she pronounced. We, too, need to strengthen our language if we want to create powerful scripts and be inspiring leaders.

Weak Language Patterns Women Use

The following patterns are ones women use often—and they make us sound unsure of ourselves.

- *We ask permission to speak when there is no need to.* For example, a woman might say, "Do you mind if I add something?" rather than *just saying it*. The notion that you're merely adding on to what others have said—and asking whether you can even do so—casts you as a subordinate.

- *We apologize far too much.* We do it in our voicemail greetings, "I'm sorry I'm not able to take your call," or "I'm sorry I'm not here." Women do this when they enter a conversation, as in *"Excuse me;* I'd like to comment on Jim's point." Or, when someone comes around the corner and there is a near-collision, who apologizes and steps aside? Typically, the woman. A woman in our seminar told us that this point really resonated with her: "I often apologized when introducing a difficult topic or when approaching someone who had other priorities. I've stopped apologizing so much."

- *We often ask questions when we know the answers.* An astonishing *80 percent* of women say they prefer to ask questions even when they know the answer.[2] Why? If they want to be collaborative, they may say, "These numbers are right, aren't they?" when they know they *are* right. One executive said to her staff member, "Are you comfortable that the audience will be able to relate to those particular messages in your presentation?" What she really wanted to say was,

"Your messages need to be clearer and more relevant for this audience." But because she didn't want to offend, she turned a statement into a question. A woman might also ask, "Do you think it would be possible for you to . . ." when asking her team member to do something, rather than saying, "I'd like you to . . ." At other times women follow every statement with "Do you know what I mean?" or "Isn't that right?" or "You know?" or "Okay?" Though such questions are intended to get reinforcement from their listener, they make the speaker sound unsure.

- *We frequently use modifiers that weaken our tone.* The worst kind are "mincing modifiers," such as *just*—as in "I'd *just* like to say something." We also use "a little bit," as in "I'm *a little bit* concerned." Or *only* and *maybe* as in "It's *only* a thought, but *maybe* we should . . ." We use "wiggle words" such as *perhaps, probably, basically, hopefully, sort of,* or *quite.* All these modifiers make women sound tentative and unsure of themselves. It's best not to use too many modifiers *at all,* because words like *very, definitely, truly, largely, always* take away from the word they're modifying. Think about it: saying "I'm definitely ready to take the stage" is less strong than "I am ready to take the stage."

- *We favor softer verbs.* We say, "I *think* there is something we can learn," rather than, "I'm *confident*/I *know* there is something we can learn." We say, "I *guess*" rather than admitting that we know something. We say, "I'll *try* to" and "I'll *attempt* to" far too often. And we use "I hope," "I feel," and "I trust"—all of which sound weak. Saying at the end of an email, "I *hope* this proposal meets your needs," suggests that you aren't sure it does—not a message you want to pass on to a customer. And saying, "I *feel* that we should do this . . ." sounds as though you don't really know whether we *should* do this. Instead, say, "I am convinced that we should do this" or simply "We should do this." Women claim to be "not sure," even when they *are* sure, and they weaken their verbs even more when they have to ask someone to do something. For example, a female store manager asking a subordinate to replace some stock might use prefatory statements like "Maybe you could . . ." Who comes across as the subordinate?

- *We use past tense . . . when we mean present.* We likely do this so as not to sound too definitive. For example, a woman might soften her introduction to a difficult discussion by saying, "I just *wanted* to spend a few minutes with you" rather than "I *want* to spend a few minutes with you." Or she might introduce her point at a meeting by saying, "I *thought* we might discuss" rather than "We should discuss . . .": or begin an email with: "I *felt* I should touch base with you." When we use the past tense it's as though we are no longer committed to what we are saying or doing. Yet of course that is not true. We just use the past to soften our style.
- *We use prefatory qualifiers that undercut our credibility.* Before making a statement, women often say, "You may already know this, but . . ." Or, "I'm not sure you're aware . . ." Or, "It's only my opinion," or "I could be wrong." Or the one we've heard thousands of times: "This is probably a stupid question, but . . ." Why diminish your credibility, and introduce your statements with words that encourage others not to take you seriously?
- *We often use a caveat after making a strong statement or a request.* We do this as a way of pulling back and not wanting to sound *too* strong. For example, "I want you to work as a team—if you are comfortable with that." Or, "We can offer you a package; but I'll have to check on that." Or, "My experience has been positive, but I don't know if statistics bear this out." Around the offices of The Humphrey Group we spend a lot of time listening to each other and making sure we practice what we teach. My assistant would never say, "I have a few things I'd like to go over with you, unless you'd like to do it another time." She would simply state, "I have a few things I'd like to discuss with you," and I will certainly find time.
- *We use emotional words that undermine us.* If you're thanking your staff for a well-done project, don't say, "I'm *happy* about it," or "With *all my heart*, I want to thank you. You can't imagine how *thankful I feel*." Just say "Thank you." Women use the word *need* more frequently than men—as in, "I *need* you to do this for me." Portraying yourself as needy does not convey a leadership image.
- *We sound overly grateful.* There is nothing wrong with being grateful or expressing gratitude, but overdoing it can make you sound weak. For

example, I received a note from someone I had helped with a job opportunity who wrote, "I just want to thank you so very much for being so supportive these past few months. You have no idea how much it has meant to me. I have not heard yet about the job, but regardless, you have been incredibly helpful and I hope you know how much it has meant to me." This lavish praise can backfire by making the sender sound as though she feels unworthy.

- *We use "I" in ways that can undermine our leadership.* In all cultures, women use "I," "me," and "mine" more than men do.[3] And the overuse of "I" does not test well. Research indicates that individuals with lower status use "I" much more frequently than those of higher rank.[4] One CFO told me that a director used "I" so many times in a one-hour discussion that it led him to conclude she was not promotable.

  "I" also has to be used with political sensitivity. I have heard of cases where ambitious men and women went to their bosses and said, "I want your job." One disappeared from the firm shortly thereafter and the other was described as "aggressive" by her boss. You must be careful to use "I" in a way that supports rather than undermines your leadership goals. Using "I" can be very effective for a leader, especially when you want to show your convictions—as in "I am convinced that our proposal is strong." But using "I" in a self-centered way ("I've done so much for the company" and "I deserve more" or "I am working so hard") can weaken your image.

The language patterns described in this chapter go a long way toward explaining why others don't hear us or take us seriously when we speak. A woman in one of our courses cleverly and with good humor summed up this topic of minimizing language and said, "I'm sorry. I was just wondering if maybe we could talk a little bit more about minimizing language, if that's okay with everyone else. I'm sorry. This may sound silly, but I just don't think I understand what minimizing language is." Everyone in the class roared, because she had beautifully captured exactly what the class was talking about.

Edit Your Language

The easiest way to begin editing your language is to listen to yourself. Notice how many times you rely on the expressions mentioned. You can begin eliminating them once you become aware of them. A woman named Glenda in our seminar apologized at least two dozen times during the first few hours of the course. If she got within three feet of anyone she said, "I'm sorry." She apologized if she spoke at the same time as anyone else in the workshop and gave them the floor. If she brushed against someone else's chair, she was contrite. Once she apologized to an empty chair that she bumped into. Glenda fortunately had a lot of support from the other women in the workshop, who smiled whenever she said, "I'm sorry." Glenda became painfully aware of her apologies—rolling her eyes whenever she uttered one. By the end of the course she had completely edited out this expression.

Another participant who wanted to speak with stronger language shared a valuable strategy: rehearse in advance. She explained, "Every week I have calls with my senior leadership team, and I notice that I've gotten a lot more confident since this training. I'm working to eliminate those weak verbs like 'I think' and 'I hope.' While I'm not quite there yet, I go over what I am going to say the day before those calls, so I can remove some of the doubt from my language and sound more confident."

The challenge at hand is to remember these weak expressions, listen to yourself, and edit them out of your script whenever you hear them. Get rid of:

- *Statements* in which you ask permission to speak.
- *Apologies*, when there's no need to be sorry.
- *Questions* for which you already have the answers.
- *Mincing modifiers*—like *just, only, quite, a bit, perhaps mostly, pretty.*
- *Too many modifiers*—like *very, truly, definitely, actually.*
- *Soft verbs* like "I'll try," "I want," "I need"—and above all, "I THINK."
- *Past tense* when you really mean present tense.
- *Prefatory qualifiers*. If you say something, say it; don't preface it with a disclaimer.
- *Caveats*. Don't say something and then undercut it.
- *Emotional words.*
- *Excessive thanks.*
- *Poor use of "I."*

You'll no longer sound like this when giving a performance review to an employee: "I want to say that I think you've done a pretty good job this year. You had to deal with some performance issues among your team members, but I am not entirely sure about that, is it true? Perhaps I could hear your views. Okay?" Edited, the passage will sound like this: "You have done an impressive job this year. You've dealt with some performance issues among your team members. I'd like to hear your views."

One woman who found this lesson on language very powerful wrote to us after the session and said, "For years, I used to watch a show called *What Not to Wear*. The show was designed to help fully capable people (mostly women) transform themselves with a new wardrobe, nice shoes, and most importantly, a new zest for life. I can't help but draw some similarities between the show and what I've learned from your language instruction. Since that session I've become horribly self-conscious about The Words Not to Wear. Choosing our language is like choosing our clothes; we *wear* our words. And we need to 'prune' our wardrobe to get rid of those words that don't make us look and sound smart, confident, and capable." As Avivah Wittenberg-Cox writes in her book *How Women Mean Business*, "Women use all kinds of vocabulary that when men listen to it, the interpretation they make of it is that it's not leadership potential material."[5]

If the opening quotation in this chapter were strengthened, it would sound like this: "I was apologetic and cautious, undercutting myself rather than sounding certain. Now I am more forthright." Let this be a call to action for all women. You have powerful ways to rewrite the language of your script. Think about the fact that every time you speak, you have the opportunity to position yourself and your ideas strongly. It's your choice.

Use strong words so others believe in you and what you are saying. And for those mentors, sponsors, and men who are reading this book—listen well, and provide clear and constructive feedback to women, so that their language sounds strong and convincing. There just might be some men on your team who can use this advice too!

Advice for Leaders of Women

Women often use minimizing words and phrases (*just* and *a little bit*), caveats ("I could be wrong" or "It's only a thought"), and weak verbs

("I think" and "I suppose"). They also ask questions when they know the answer and apologize when there's no need to. Women tend to speak this way to create a tone of modesty and self-effacement. But such language does not serve them well as leaders. What can you do to help?

- Study this chapter to discover the weak expressions many women use.
- Ask yourself, "Do women use these words more often than men?"
- If you hear such tentativeness, take the individual aside, explain what you have observed, and help her understand how these phrases can undercut her credibility.
- Provide training that helps her speak as a stronger leader.

Chapter Eleven

Structure Your Script

Creating a strong, well-argued script is not a skill we learn in school, or in most leadership courses. I learned this craft from Roy Cottier, my first boss. After he hired me fresh out of university teaching, he began grooming me to become an executive speech writer—preparing talks for our CEO and other executives. It was a steep learning curve, and I remember tossing my first speech into his in-basket and walking as fast as I could back to my office so I wouldn't have to see him reading it. But no sooner had I arrived in the safety of my small space than the phone rang and he said (with an uncharacteristic note of warmth in his voice), "You've made it!" Cottier mentored me and made clear that a well-argued script is message driven. And he showed me that message and structure were needed, not just for formal speeches, but for every communication.

This chapter will show you how to create clear, well-structured scripts. No matter how powerful your ideas or how confident your delivery, you'll get no buy-in from your audience if you can't convey your thoughts in a persuasive way. The methodology presented in this chapter is The Leader's Script®, developed and branded by The Humphrey Group. It will enable you to organize your thoughts and stay with them until you have convinced others. Use this template to structure your ideas—whether you're making a presentation or having an elevator conversation. It provides your roadmap to persuasive leadership.

Design of the Script

The Leader's Script is an extraordinary tool for both men and women. But for women it is particularly important because it counters our tendency to soften our messages rather than speaking in a forthright manner. As Agrium CFO Stephen Dyer said, "Women tend to use a more questioning communication style, whereas men are more direct. A woman might say, 'Do you think this would work?' rather than, 'Here is the way I believe things need to be.'"

The Leader's Script will give you more control of your message. In fact, it will show you how to state your message up front and develop it successfully. You'll come across as taking a position and driving it home.

Here's the template. You can download an electronic version of this template at The Humphrey Group's website.[1]

The Leader's Script®

Grabber: _____

Subject: _____

Message: _____

Structural
Statement: _____

Point One: _____

Point Two: _____

Point Three: _____

Restated
Message: _____

Call to Action: _____

Your message is at the heart of The Leader's Script. State it near the beginning, develop it in the body, and restate it near the end. The template ensures that you will get your message across to your audience by using each of the following elements to your advantage.

Grabber

The grabber is the opening element that enables you to engage your audience. Think of it as a verbal handshake that "grabs" your audience's attention and brings them closer to you. It can be about you ("I"), your audience ("you"), or something you and your audience share ("we"). Here are some sample grabbers that you can adapt to your own remarks:

- *"I" grabbers:* "*I've* thought a lot about this issue/challenge/your performance/our debate/discussion," or "*I'm* so proud to be here to accept this award," or "*I* am delighted with the success our team has delivered this year."
- *"You" grabbers:* "*You* in this room have made a strong case," or "*You* have turned in a solid performance." Or, "Good morning, *everyone.*"
- *"We" grabbers:* "*All of us* here have one purpose," or "*You and I* are in agreement," or (in a team meeting) "*We* need to find a solution."

The length of the grabber will depend upon the situation. For a formal speech or presentation it might be up to a minute. For example, the "Good morning *everyone*" example could be developed into "Good morning everyone. Hasn't this been a great conference!" The leader would then continue the grabber with highlights of that event, thereby building excitement and shared vision. For informal remarks, the grabber is more likely to be just a sentence or two.

Subject

The subject follows the grabber and presents your topic. It's a statement that begins with "I'd like to look at . . ." or "I want to discuss . . ." or "I'm writing to you about . . ." (You don't need this subject statement if the subject is already clear.)

Message

The most critical element of a leader's script is the message, as it is your *main* point. It should be an idea or argument based on your convictions. If you don't have a message, your audience will be asking themselves, "Why should I be listening?" "Where is this going?" "What is the point?" "Why does this concern me?" The message is not a factual statement: it is a leadership statement—something you believe and that you're going to prove. So frame your message with words and phrases like:

- "I believe that . . ."
- "I'm convinced that . . ."
- "My message is . . ."
- "My point is . . ."
- "I suggest that . . ."
- "As I see it . . ."

Having a message will give you enormous credibility. Whether you are speaking to a board of directors or to your boss, your audience wants to know that you are saying *something* to them—not just rambling. When they hear your message, they'll be thinking "Ah! *There's* the point."

Structural Statement

The structural statement, which is the last element in the introduction, provides an *overview* of your structure. If you intend to take your audience through a set of reasons to prove your message, your structural statement might sound like this: "I'll give you three reasons why I believe this." If you want to describe a challenge, then a response to that challenge, your structural statement would be, "I'll first discuss the challenge we face, then I'll outline our solution." This element makes it easier for listeners to follow you. You're giving them a "roadmap" of the structure.

Body of Script

Once you've given your audience a sense of your structure, proceed to the body of your script. This is where you sell your message by providing a set of arguments that will lead your audience to the same conclusion you have drawn. To create your main proof points, choose one of the following patterns of organization.

- *Reasons.* This pattern sets forth the reasons your message is valid.
- *Ways.* This pattern shows the ways your message is true.
- *Situation/Response.* This pattern shows first a situation, challenge, or opportunity, and then your response or solution to that situation.
- *Present Results/Future Prospects.* This "update" structure first discusses what's happened to date, and then what you envision in the future.
- *Chronological.* This structure is a step-by-step structure in which the points reflect stages in a process or events over time.

You can choose whichever pattern best elaborates or proves your message.

To keep your audience focused on each main point, flag them. Let's say you're using reasons. When you come to the first point, say, "The first reason I believe . . ." or "First, I believe . . ." or simply, "First . . ." When you come to each of your other points do the same thing. This reference to "first, second, and third" will keep both speaker and audience aware of which proof point you're delivering. Otherwise, points tend to bleed into each other—and you don't want that to happen. You want to be clear, with each point contributing to a strong, persuasive argument.

If your script is for something more than a thirty-second elevator conversation or answer to a question, you will want to flesh out your main proof points—and you will need subpoints to do so. The process for developing subpoints is the same as for your main points; choose a pattern for each set of subpoints. The sample scripts in the next few chapters show how that works.

Restated Message

After your proof points, bring your audience back to your message. For example, you might say, "So you can see we're on course to deliver our key initiatives."

Call to Action

Your message, once proven, should lead to action. It can be an action you undertake or one you ask your audience to take. Too few speakers ask their audience to act—but leaders do! So, tell your audience what they need to do. ("I look forward to your approval and funding for this project," or, "Let's stay the course, and support each other on this initiative until we have succeeded in delivering it to our internal clients.") Don't say—as so many people do at the end of their emails—"If you have any questions, do not hesitate to call me." This is what I call a "limping" call to action.

These are all the elements of The Leader's Script. Using this template ensures that you will have a grabber, a clear message, proof points, and a call to action every time you speak. There is no guarantee that you will always deliver this type of script uninterrupted; during an off-the-cuff meeting, job interview, or conversation, you'll likely deliver your script in stages, and through give and take. But if you keep your script in mind the entire time, you will eventually move through all your proof points to the conclusion. Every time you use the script you will come across as prepared and insightful. So, burn it in your mind.

If you want a voice at the table, you'll need to bring your thinking forward clearly and decisively. Organizations need both male and female thought leaders, and conveying clear thinking is the essence of thought leadership. The following three chapters will show you how to apply The Leader's Script in a broad range of situations. It will not only make you sound smart and savvy; it will turn your listeners into believers.

Advice for Leaders of Women

You will want those on your team to influence. One important way they can do this is to have a strong script. What can you do to encourage this?

- Read this chapter and discover the power of The Leader's Script.
- Ask yourself, "Do my team members speak with a clear message?" "Are they convincing in getting across their point?" "Do they end with a call to action?"
- Coach your team members in these fundamentals.

Chapter Twelve

Master Meeting Scripts

I n one of our seminars, Sophia, an insurance company manager, prepared a script to deliver in a meeting with her boss. Her message to him was, "I am absolutely confident that all three options I am putting in front of you today will lead to a positive outcome." After taking the class through the three options, she came back to her message, "So as you can see all three of these options really will lead to a wonderful solution."

Our instructor approached her during the break to give her private feedback and asked, "Just between the two of us, which one of these options do you think is the best?"

"Oh, definitely option two," Sophia replied instantly.

"What if your script were to say, 'I am convinced that option two is the best approach for us to take—and here are the reasons why'?" our instructor asked.

"I guess I could try that," Sophia said. So together they wrote it out— and Sophia delivered that stronger, message-based script. Two weeks later her boss called the instructor.

"You had one of my employees in your Taking the Stage course a few weeks ago," he said, "and I don't know what you did, but for the first time in thirty years I am getting my money's worth from her."

A good script delivers *a forceful message*, not just options for others to consider. Sophia's success reflected the powerful script she developed. This chapter discusses crafting scripts for three meeting situations. As you'll see, The Leader's Script will enable you to come across as a focused and persuasive leader.

Formal Meeting Talks

Formal meetings are important events for you and those listening to you. These occasions could include a presentation to the board or a speech to a sales team. Depending on the corporate culture, you might use slides.

With a formal talk to a large group it's often best to craft fully written remarks. For example, if you are making a speech or delivering a presentation to three hundred people at an industry event, create your talk by amplifying The Leader's Script with a group of paragraphs to support each point. That way, you know every word you're going to speak. If your formal talk is to a smaller group, you can create a simpler set of talking points using this template.

In the following example The Leader's Script is used to create a formal talk for a company retreat. The speaker is a manager who is addressing her salespeople about the importance of teamwork in selling. Her wonderful personal grabber creates an excellent bridge to her clear and well-developed message. It is an inspiring talk.

GRABBER: Years ago, a new salesperson joined our firm. She was determined to beat everyone else and be tops in sales at the end of her first year. She wanted to achieve this completely on her own without anyone's help. Well, she ended up with *lower* sales than anyone else at the end of that first year. Do you know how I know this? I know it, because that person was me.

SUBJECT: I'm here today to talk to you about a better approach to selling.

MESSAGE: I believe that it's only through teamwork that our sales team will achieve our best sales numbers.

STRUCTURAL STATEMENT: I'll first explain why teamwork is so essential for us; then I'll talk about how we're going to improve our performance

POINT 1: Teamwork is critical to our sales success.

- It will allow us to bring our broad portfolio to clients.
- It will enable us to find the best solutions.
- It will give clients an appreciation for our team.

POINT 2: Teamwork will take concerted effort on our part.

- We must forget our egos.
- We must make introductions.
- We must work collaboratively.

RESTATED MESSAGE: If we do these things, we will have much better sales.

CALL TO ACTION: We will also have a much better team—one I know I can count on to deliver exceptional and sustainable results.

Imagine yourself giving a talk like this—one that conveys a new vision for your team and generates excitement about what's possible. Your theme could be anything from a new strategy to a client opportunity. This structure provides an excellent template. So next time you give a major talk, come back to this example and see whether you can build upon it.

Informal Meeting Remarks

In contrast to formal talks, informal remarks are typically delivered in everyday meetings, and the speaker has less time to prepare. You may have only a few hours—or a few minutes—to pull together your thoughts. In such informal remarks you might update a group on a project or report on recent sales figures.

The following examples suggest how to use The Leader's Script to create your informal meeting remarks—in three different modes. In this first example, an HR manager prepares to update her boss on projects that are under way. The script takes the form of an outline that will be expanded as the manager speaks. Note the brevity of the script and how it positions her accomplishments.

GRABBER: How are you? It's been a while since we've gotten together.

SUBJECT: I have lots to update you on.

MESSAGE: I'm pleased to say that all our initiatives are moving forward nicely.

STRUCTURAL STATEMENT: I'll take you through the three main ones.

POINT 1: First, the employee engagement survey is in excellent shape.

POINT 2: Second, our succession planning is progressing well.

POINT 3: Third, although we've had some setbacks on the hiring front, I expect we will be able to fill the outstanding positions in the new year.

RESTATED MESSAGE: So you can see we are on course with our key initiatives.

CALL TO ACTION: I am confident they will come through on time, on budget, and in keeping with our goals.

In this next example of an informal meeting script, Penny, a thirty-one-year-old manager on her bank's trading floor, writes out her script verbatim and memorizes it on the train while riding to work. She does this to make sure she knows *exactly* what to tell the other traders about upcoming opportunities.

GRABBER: Good morning, everyone.

MESSAGE: This morning I am going to highlight three opportunities we have over the next month.

POINT 1: The first and most important is with Union Energy. We are underwriters in this bought deal. This is our top pick of any US energy firm. They'll be in Toronto and Montreal, and we have spots available for you to meet with the CEO in both cities.

POINT 2: Second, the London team will be hosting an agricultural conference on the 21st. With more than ten companies presenting, we have one-on-one meetings available with several firms.

POINT 3: Third, we have an opportunity for those interested in income trusts. This is a sector outperformer—great for a high yield low risk play. We have the 9:45 slot available in New York on Wednesday.

CALL TO ACTION: Let me know if you'd like to participate in any of these opportunities.

Informal meeting scripts can take a third form: a brief outline quickly jotted down on the back of a business card or noted on a smartphone. A young banker told me she used this approach:

I was at a conference in London, and my team wanted to persuade clients to do business with us. We saw an opportunity and we were the only Canadian dealer in that space. So I stepped away from the conference and spent the break working on a brief pitch. I jotted down a few notes on the back of a business card—and I burned the outline into my mind. And it worked! We have two new major European accounts.

My *message* was that we are the Canadian leader in the field, and my *proof points* showed (1) our historical strength; (2) our present leadership and global reach; (3) our strong client relationships; and (4) our willingness to offer pricing incentives. The *call to action* was that because of our unique strengths we would bring value to their business.

You have here three different example of informal meeting scripts. Next time you have an informal meeting at which you intend to speak up, come back to this chapter and decide which format you want to use. And make sure you have the strong message and key points that will make your remarks powerful!

Off-the-Cuff Meeting Remarks

Much of the speaking we do in meetings falls under the heading of "off-the-cuff" or "impromptu" comments. You might be called upon for an update on a project or an answer to a question. The key for successful impromptu remarks is to use The Leader's Script to collect your thoughts *before* speaking. One woman we worked with lamented that most people didn't listen to her at meetings. But upon reflection she realized that she "just jumped in with the content, spoke too fast, and was unfocused." Now she thinks through her message before speaking and has greatly improved her ability to get her point across.

Let's say you're in a meeting, and a colleague asks you, as the finance person in the room, "How do our numbers look for this quarter?" Instead of panicking, pause and respond as follows.

GRABBER: I'm glad you asked.
MESSAGE: We've had a strong fourth quarter.
STRUCTURAL STATEMENT: [None needed.]

POINT 1: Revenue is up 5 percent over the same period last year.

POINT 2: And costs have held steady—increasing only 1 percent year over year.

RESTATED MESSAGE: So it's been a profitable quarter.

CALL TO ACTION: We remain on track for a banner year.

The examples in this chapter suggest the many ways you can use this template during meetings. And the more you use it, the more agile you will be at creating meeting scripts of all kinds—formal, informal, and off-the-cuff. These scripts will make you sound confident and clear, and allow you to hold the attention of everyone in the room. A strong script creates a memorable impression of who you are and what you do. It will allow you to inspire your listeners.

Advice for Leaders of Women

Meetings are one of the most important settings for men and women who wish to move their careers forward. In meetings people get heard—or don't; they influence—or don't; they show themselves as thought leaders—or don't. And the scripts they deliver, whether in the form of text or mental notes, can make all the difference. Help women express themselves with more confidence and clarity in meetings in the following ways:

- Listen to them—don't tune them out just because they may not be communicating in a style you would use. Women's desire to be inclusive may lead to a more "leisurely" route to their point.
- Ask yourself how persuasive they are. Do they have a message? Do they support it with proof points?
- Observe whether they stay on message, or whether they back off too quickly, or "fold" in the face of opposition. If they do back off, help them get back on track by stepping in and reinforcing their point—showing others in the room that this individual has said something significant.
- Consider whether in their project updates to you, female direct reports have a message or high-level vision about each project. Or do they provide excessive detail in an effort to prove that they have worked hard?

- If you find women need coaching in any of these areas, counsel them. Ask them to read this chapter and apply what they learn. Provide regular feedback and encouragement.
- When a woman does make a strong case or progresses in this area, show a willingness to "buy into" her ideas—even if it means changing direction yourself.

Chapter Thirteen

Craft Career Conversations

One of my own defining career conversations took place at lunch with an actor, Marshall Bell, who was in Toronto to coach our bank's executives in how to deliver their remarks. As the firm's speech writer, I was hosting him at a quaint little seafood restaurant. It would have been easy to sit back and let Marshall regale me with stories about his roles in *Stand by Me*, *Twins*, *Total Recall*, *Digstown*, and *Star Troopers*. But because I had been thinking about launching a firm that would teach executives how to speak, the coaching he was providing to the bank's executives greatly interested me—so I probed. As I listened, the thought flashed through my mind that we would make a good team. So I said to Marshall, "Why don't we start a company? I'll teach executives how to write great speeches, and you can teach them how to deliver them!" I sketched a business plan on a napkin. That was the moment I first conceived of The Humphrey Group. To this day, our firm continues to teach what I envisioned at that lunch—how to create great scripts and deliver them with presence.

This story illustrates that if you want to move ahead in your career, you have to focus on the next opportunity and see *every conversation* as a chance to explore what's possible. When I had lunch that day with Marshall, I was so intent on launching a business that I jumped at what

I knew was the perfect chance to do so. In this chapter you will discover how to create scripts that advance your career. These include networking scripts, exchanges with your sponsor, job interviews, and discussions with your boss. In every case, The Leader's Script will enable you to make a strong case for yourself.

Networking Conversations

Networking events provide an excellent opportunity to meet new people and explore ways to move your career forward. Cathryn Gabor, then SVP of human resources for a global company, told me how a breakfast gathering helped her advance her career:

> Greg, the speaker and managing director of a global executive search firm, stood up at an HR networking event and asked each of us to share our goals. I began to mentally script myself with words like "I am at a turning point in my career; I am about to leave my employer, and frankly I am interested in Africa and animals." But on reflection I realized that such a script would get me nowhere professionally. I had a huge opportunity standing before me. So when it was my turn, I said, "My name is Cathryn Gabor and I am the head of HR for my firm. I see myself moving into executive search with a company like Greg's. This field interests me for several reasons. First, I began my career in sales and would like to use my business development skills in such a role. Second, I have talent management expertise that's critical in the search business. And finally, recruiting has always been a core strength of mine; I have always been able to assess and place A-players, and in some senses, my career has been building to the executive search and leadership consulting industry."

Following the presentation, Greg told Cathryn that he liked her energy, passion, and skills, and his firm had an opening for a partner in her city. Greg introduced her to his colleagues—sponsoring her—and she was interviewed over a two-month period, after which she was offered—and accepted—what she saw as the "position of a lifetime."

At the heart of this successful case study is The Leader's Script. Cathryn positioned herself professionally with a grabber ("My name is Cathryn Gabor and I am head of HR for my firm"); a message ("I see myself moving into executive search with a company like Greg's"); a structure that developed her message (three reasons why she is ready to take on that assignment); and a call to action ("My career has been building to executive search"). She and Greg then used the follow-up conversation to "close" on this opportunity.

Conversation with a Sponsor

Another important script for anyone seeking to advance her career is one directed to a sponsor or influential executive. These high-ranking individuals are critical to your career, so don't treat such conversations lightly. For example, you wouldn't approach a potential sponsor in a cafeteria and casually say, "I am looking around for a job—and I'm open to suggestions. Do you know of anything?" That would be far too informal and unfocused. The proper way to approach a sponsor involves the following two-step process: set up a meeting and then have a positive conversation. Alexis is the young woman profiled here.

Step 1: Alexis Sets Up the Meeting

Grabber: Tom, I'm glad to see you. I've been thinking about giving you a call to ask if you'd have time to sit down with me sometime during the next few weeks.

Subject: I'd like to talk with you about the next step in my career.

Message: You have always given me great advice, and there is an opportunity I'd like to pursue with your guidance.

After getting a positive response, Alexis continues . . .

Call to Action: I'll talk to your assistant about a setting up a time for us to talk. Thank you and I look forward to our conversation.

Step 2: Alexis Meets with Tom

Grabber: Thanks for meeting with me, Tom. I have been doing a lot of thinking about the next step in my career, and your opinion really matters to me.

Subject: I want to talk to you about a possibility that interests me—a position that is opening up in London, in Jim Ketch's organization.

Message: I believe it represents an excellent fit with my goals and abilities.

Structural Statement: There are a number of reasons I say that.

Point 1: It would give me international experience.

Point 2: It would play to my strengths as a people leader.

Point 3: I have the knowledge of corporate finance they want.

Restated Message: So it's an attractive fit.

Call to Action: I would like to pursue this opportunity. Would you be willing to put my name forward to Jim? I know he values your advice.

What makes this a successful exchange?

- Alexis uses the first conversation to *set up a meeting* with Tom. He will be ready for what she has to say and will appreciate that she gives him advance notice.
- She comes across as having a thoughtful, long-term career focus.
- She has a carefully crafted script that sells her into the position.
- She is politically savvy—she shows respect for Tom's views and reinforces that Jim respects Tom's opinions too.
- She comes across as confident, professional, and worthy.
- She asks him to sponsor her in her call to action. Notice that she makes this request in the form of a question. While this may sound tentative on the surface, it's an excellent and positive way to close—by asking "for the sale."

This example beautifully illustrates how to take the stage with a sponsor.

Conversation with an Employer

Sponsors open doors, but prospective employers provide jobs. So carefully prepare for your job interview by creating a winning script. *Never* say, "I'm not sure I am right for this position; I only have *some* of the qualifications you are looking for." You need to fully promote yourself if you want the job. Create and memorize a script that explains why you are an excellent fit for the position. Use the situation/response structure in the following example. The situation (Point 1) is your description of the opportunity, and the response (Point 2) is your explanation of how you fit the opportunity.

Grabber: Thank you for this opportunity to meet with you.
Subject: I am pleased to be considered for this position.
Message: It interests me greatly, and I believe my skills fit well with what you are looking for.
Structural Statement: [None required here, because message provides sense of structure.]
Point 1: I'm attracted to this position for several reasons.
- Your bank has always impressed me.
- I understand that you're creating a retail bank with a new level of service.
- The position would have a large sphere of influence.
Point 2: I believe I am well suited to the role.
- My values dovetail with your bank's culture.
- I have overseen a transformation similar to the one under way in your retail bank.
- Leadership is an important requirement of the job, and I see myself as a strong leader.
Restated Message: I believe my background fits well with the requirements of the position.
Call to Action: I look forward to the prospect of working for your firm and making a long-term commitment. What are the next steps?

Next time you have a job interview, come back to this script and use it to design your own. The content will change, but the structure is an excellent one for showing *why* you are attracted to the position and *how* you will deliver.

Conversation with Your Manager

Some of the most important career conversations you'll have are with your boss. It's up to you to convince her or him to be your champion. You need to initiate these discussions. Teresa, a regional finance manager of a global logistics company, did just that. She took the stage and spoke to her boss about a potential opportunity. Although he was initially skeptical, she persisted. As the following dialogue suggests, she created a script that persuaded him.

[Teresa]

Grabber: I hear there is a possibility of another controller position opening up in the United States.
Subject: I would like to apply for the position.
Message: I believe I have the qualifications for it.

[Manager]

I don't think you're ready.

[Teresa]

Can you tell me why?

[Manager]

[He gives the reasons she may not have the qualifications.]

[Teresa]

Grabber: Well, let me get the job description and we can go through what's required.
Message: I believe you'll see I meet the requirements. *[She brings forward the job description.]*
Point 1: I have the years of experience they are looking for.
Point 2: I have the controller background.
Point 3: They're looking for certification—and I have that.
Point 4: I have the relationship-building skills—proven in my present role.
Restated Message: There appears to be a good fit, don't you agree?

[Manager]

Call to Action: I can see your reasoning. Although I'd hate to lose you, I think you should apply. You have my support.

By using The Leader's Script, Teresa stayed true to her message and structured the conversation by supporting it with reasons. She could have gotten angry, upset, or discouraged when her boss initially disagreed. But she stayed focused. In the end he was swayed by her strong case, and he, too, deserves credit for coming around. This dialogue also shows that if you have a good script, you can present your main points while being a responsive listener. The script will ground you.

This chapter has shown how to initiate and engage in conversations that move your career forward. Landing a job or that next promotion depends on successfully scripting yourself and on having a clear idea of *where you want to be next.* Don't think your organization is all knowing or has a plan for your next move. It's *your* job to have that plan. So get focused on what you want to do and be sure you are prepared to discuss this next step when you approach sponsors, prospective employers, or your manager. Doing so will give you yet another opportunity to take the stage.

Advice for Leaders of Women

It is crucial for women to represent themselves well in career discussions. You can provide direction and encouragement to help them.

- Develop a "visibility plan" for women. Talk to the women in advance about how they can best represent themselves when networking internally.
- Create opportunities for women in your organization to network with senior executives. For example, you might host a gathering for women in your group and invite executives from other divisions or invite your boss or CEO.
- Spend one-on-one time with women whom you see as having career potential. Chat about their career goals—help them identify next steps and future possibilities. Let them know you support them in this journey.

- When career opportunities open up, coach them on interview skills, on selling themselves and delivering strong, clear messages about themselves.
- Never stand in the way of a career opportunity. In fact, fully support and "go to bat" for deserving individuals, and use your influence to advance a strong candidate.
- Remember: Women often feel excluded and overlooked and need your support.

Chapter Fourteen

Elevate Your Elevator Scripts

A managing director named Simone told me that the most important thing she learned about taking the stage is how to deal
with elevator conversations. She explained, "If you happen to be in the
elevator with the head of your firm, don't just say, 'What do you think of
the weather?' Take the opportunity to say, 'Our group is having a great
year. Revenue is up, margins are better, and we've had several big wins.'
Use those conversations to pitch yourself internally to your colleagues.
This is especially important when you work for a large organization."

Simone saw the power of these brief, impromptu exchanges and was
able to deliver clear, crisp scripts that boosted her stock and that of her
team. These "small stages" provide great opportunities. Though we often
label them "elevator conversations," they include the chats that take
place in corridors, coffee rooms, parking lots, or anywhere else there is
informal mingling.

Learning how to use these moments effectively is a wonderful business skill. According to Catalyst's report, "Unwritten Rules," the "top
unwritten rules to advancement" include two all-important actions:
(1) "network and build relationships within and outside the corporation," and (2) "find ways to become visible."[1] Elevator conversations
help you in both areas. You can become visible to those you might not

otherwise meet—the elevator is the great equalizer! And you can use those brief moments of conversation to build relationships. To succeed, you need to focus your thinking, "read" the opportunity, and use The Leader's Script.

Focus Your Thinking

This is something you should do long before the elevator doors open. The best way to prepare for these brief chats is to have some key messages in your mind all the time—about your major wins, your client projects, your management achievements, and your personal successes. It's not possible to talk this way unless you think this way, so make these positive messages part of your mindset. The managing director in the chapter's opening story did not suddenly realize in the elevator that her group's revenue was up, margins were better, and her team had several wins. She thinks about these things all the time, so those messages came to her quickly at the very moment she needed to cite them.

Then, focus on those powerful messages once you are faced with such an opportunity. Even if you're having a challenging day, and someone asks, "How's it going?" don't say, "Oh, terribly!" Rather, tell yourself, "I can deliver a crucial message to the person who has just stepped into the elevator." By thinking in those terms, you'll find you'll be able to create a powerful script.

Read the Room

Reading the room in the case of an elevator ride or a corridor conversation involves several things. First, ask yourself if the setting is right to deliver a message. If the elevator is crowded or there are people present who shouldn't hear what you would like to say, it may not be the best time. In that case, simply say "Hello" or smile to that individual. Second, decide whether the individual you would like to talk to seems approachable; does his or her body language indicate self-containment or openness? If the person's arms are folded and his head is down, save your conversation for another day. But if that individual gives you a warm look, take the opportunity to engage in a chat. Third, determine what kind of opportunity you have—how can a conversation move your business or career agenda forward? Once you have read the opportunity, you are ready to script yourself.

Create Your Script

There are, of course, times when you just want to say "hi" to someone in the elevator. But if you want to make something of the situation and advance your business agenda, rely on the powerful architecture of The Leader's Script. And why wouldn't you? The elevator may be a small stage, but it gives you an opportunity to raise your profile and speak to people at all levels of your organization you might not otherwise encounter. If you use this template regularly for formal and informal scripts, it becomes second nature in extemporaneous situations like elevator conversations. Following are four ways you can use The Leader's Script to influence and inspire others on this small stage.

Share a Win

First, the elevator is a great place to share a success! It need not sound like boasting. Think of it simply as sharing a good news corporate story. Let's say a colleague gets in the elevator and asks, "How did the customer meeting go?" Your script might sound like the following.

GRABBER: The meeting went really well.
SUBJECT: We won the business.
MESSAGE: I'm excited about this breakthrough . . .
STRUCTURAL STATEMENT: For several reasons.
POINT 1: We will become the sole provider of IT services for this client.
POINT 2: We'll triple our revenues on this account.
POINT 3: Most important, we have a new business model we can use with other clients.
RESTATED MESSAGE: So it's an exciting development.
CALL TO ACTION: The team is energized. In fact we're off to celebrate!

Notice this script's simplicity: it's essentially a strong message and three proof points. Still, it's inspiring. And if your colleague does not ask you about the meeting, initiate the topic with a grabber like this: "I've just come from our meeting with customer X."

Be sure also to share personal wins. If you have just been chosen for an award, received a promotion, or have some other good news, don't hide your light under a bushel of self-doubts; share it with others. It may feel like boasting to you, but it will sound like confident leadership to others.

Discuss an Initiative

Second, you might discuss a business initiative. Liz Reynolds, manager of diversity for KPMG, was excited to tell me when I met her at a party that she has begun sharing such successes in elevator chats with her company's CEO. As she put it:

> I often find myself riding up forty-seven floors with our CEO. Before attending Taking the Stage, I would get nervous during those two or three minutes; I'd either stay silent or talk about the weather. Now, I think of my elevator pitch as soon as I see the CEO coming through the elevator doors. I take the opportunity to highlight something that I am doing to directly benefit the business. For example, our firm recently received client work focusing on the employment environment for New Canadians. In my last elevator chat I told the CEO that I had made personal introductions for the project team to community organizations that support new immigrants. If I hadn't told him that, he would never have known that I bring important connections to KPMG. My goal was to leave him with the confidence that I and my department are adding value.

No matter what business project you are working on, articulate your accomplishments and the other person will see that you are confident and focused on delivering for the business. Building your profile in this way is extraordinarily important to your career.

Provide an Update

Third, you can update someone on how a project is coming along. If your boss steps into the elevator or stops you in the hallway and asks, "Will you have those figures for me today?" your grabber might be, "Yes, of course," and your message, "I've made great progress putting the budget together." Then comes your structure. You don't need "first," "second," and "third" in such brief remarks, but you might have several supporting points: "I've gotten numbers from everyone in the group . . . I've consolidated them . . . And I've got a final number that will really please you because it shows we're significantly reducing costs." Always conclude with your call to action: "I'll see you at 2 p.m. and we can go over these results." You can easily create this kind of powerful script on the spot. Indeed, when you're asked, "How is Project X coming along?" just think of what you have accomplished and that will be your message. Your structure will be "ways" or "things" that define what's been done.

Build a Relationship

Fourth, the elevator is a great place to introduce yourself and build a relationship. There are times when someone you know—but who doesn't know you—will get into the elevator. If you would like them to know who you are, take the next thirty seconds to introduce yourself. The Leader's Script is an excellent template for doing so.

Suppose you are in the elevator and see an executive from another division who has supported your group. You might say, "Hello, I'm Linda Vince, manager of private banking. I want to tell you that those referrals you've been sending us have been terrific—they've helped us more than double our business. I'd love to get together to see how we can further build this partnership." There are only three elements in this short script: grabber, message, and call to action. But in this situation, it works!

Let's say you have sixty-five floors to do a full introduction. Here's one example where a new executive assistant introduces herself to her company's president.

GRABBER: Hello Mr. Montclair (extending her hand).
SUBJECT: I'm Vanessa Cartright, executive assistant to the CFO.
MESSAGE: I joined this company three months ago, and I feel very fortunate.
POINT 1: There is such a great spirit and energy here.
POINT 2: And I love working with the executive team. It's a great group of people who have made me feel very welcome.
CALL TO ACTION: I'm looking forward to your speech next week.

This new employee has just taken a step to advance her career. She has gained visibility with the CEO and conveyed her excitement about working for the organization he heads. Should the CEO see her again, or speak to her when he is trying to reach the CFO, he will remember her as a confident, committed employee. And if he ever needs an EA, who will come to mind?

The elevator and similar situations provide a host of opportunities to take the stage. Though they may be small stages, remember they give you another person's *undivided attention*. If you are skilled at reading the opportunity and delivering a short script on one of the themes discussed in this chapter, you will be able to take full advantage of this situation. You only need thirty seconds to a minute to discuss a business initiative or your progress on a project. You can build a relationship, arrange a meeting, or raise your profile. So enhance your status and "elevate" yourself using the elevator conversation.

Advice for Leaders of Women

Some of the most important conversations take place in informal settings such as elevators, corridors, and coffee rooms. You can use these situations as "mentoring moments" in the following ways:

- When you are in the elevator, corridor, or other informal situations, open up the conversation with women on your team and with others.
- Instead of the usual chit chat, ask them a question of substance—one that allows them to share success stories or business initiatives.
- Acknowledge their achievements.
- End with a call to action: "let's have coffee," or "I'd like to discuss a role you might play on that project team," or simply, "keep up the good work."

Part Three

Unlock the Power of Your Voice

Chapter Fifteen

Begin by Breathing

Voice is central to leadership. When a leader takes the stage, she puts out vocal energy that compels her audience to listen. She speaks loudly and distinctly. She knows that her leadership will be compromised if an audience has to struggle to hear or understand what she is saying. She also knows that boring her audience with a monotone voice will undermine her leadership. If she speaks with distracting vocal patterns—such as a little girl voice that's consistently too high, or a voice that rises at the end of thoughts, or if she speaks too softly—the people listening and watching won't see her as a leader. Leaders captivate their audience by using all their voice's natural talents. Part 3 of the book will help you develop that powerful instrument of leadership through breathing, volume, authenticity, pace, expression, and articulation. To begin, let's look at how you can unlock the power of your voice by tapping into your natural vocal energy—your breath.

The Importance of Breath

The deeper the breath, the more potential you have to influence an audience. To discover how closely connected breath and sound are, hold your breath and try making a sound. It's almost impossible; they are *that* closely linked. If you want your voice to be strong and deep enough to convey your passion and enthusiasm, you must connect with your breath. Indeed, the starting point of being truly present to an audience is *to breathe*.

Why We Lose Touch with Our Breath

Finding this wellspring of breath is not easy. Because many things can constrict our breath, the richness of sound that comes from deep breathing is not always evident in our voices. To begin with, women are often taught to pull in their stomachs to look more attractive—something that unfortunately constricts our breath. We often say to participants in our courses, "Would you rather have a powerful voice, or a slightly thinner figure?" It's actually a toss-up for some!

Many other things we do make it difficult for us to find our breath. If you're tense or fearful—from performance jitters or stress—you will speak without sufficient breath. If you're physically inactive, your breathing muscles may become idle and nonresponsive. Too much caffeine, too, can speed up and overwhelm our breathing center. Too much adrenalin, as well, can make us forget to breathe. Poor posture can constrict our breath. Our minds and emotions, too, can diminish our breath. If we feel a lack of conviction about our topic, we will speak with less breath. If we walk past someone who intimidates us, we may breathe very little when saying "Hi." But if we see a close friend, we may breathe deeply and bring forward an enthusiastic "I'm so glad to see you." So there are many situations in which we may not be as full of breath as we need to be to project confident leadership. We once had a participant in our seminar who got up to give her presentation and was so terrified that she could not utter a single sound. Our instructor asked her simply to breathe and slowly to make eye contact with everybody in the room, one by one. She was shaking, and our instructor said, "Just keep breathing. Say nothing, just stay with it." Slowly but surely she came through the fire, with her breathing getting deeper and deeper. By the time she reached the seventh and last person, she had become grounded and powerful, and even began to smile and connect with her audience. She said the exercise taught her that there was nothing to be afraid of, because she had a wellspring of breath that could remove her anxieties.

Finding Your Breath

There are many ways you can get in touch with your breath and create a strong and reliable source of vocal power. You can begin by doing the following exercise to help you tell the difference between shallow and deep breathing.

> Take in a breath, but take it high up in your chest and hold in your stomach muscles, like a model. Keep holding in your stomach muscles. Register how that feels. Keep holding them in. Women spent centuries in corsets that made them feel just like you're feeling right now. Now let out a big sigh, then soften all around your belly region and allow breath to again fill you up from the bottom to the top. That exercise will show you what a relaxed generous breath feels like.

Learn to appreciate that deep, free breathing. Sense how comfortable it allows you to feel in your body. Notice, too, when your breathing feels like you're wearing a too-tight corset—and see if you can figure out what situations lead to those feelings.

When you give speeches and presentations, put notations in your script or speaking notes to remind yourself to breathe. These breath marks should be at the beginning of paragraphs and in front of important sentences. Taking deep breaths often when you speak will give you a sense of control, and it will make your audience feel that you are speaking with strength and purpose. As well, the pauses these big breaths create will give you an even more confident and grounded style.

To get yourself breathing, exercise. Jog, take long walks, dance, meditate, and practice yoga—all things that are good not just for your voice but for your whole body. Maggie Huculak, one of our instructors conducting a seminar in Mexico City, had a participant named Teresa who held her breath in when she spoke. Because of that, she seemed angry. To address this issue, Maggie asked Teresa to run up and down the hallway until she was out of breath. She did so, and when she came back into the room, she was laughing and panting. *She had found her breath!* Shortly afterward, Teresa delivered her speech with more warmth and energy than she had previously shown, because she had learned how to breathe life into her communications.

Still another way to find your breath is to stand tall so you're letting your rib cage move out freely and your belly muscles relax. This body alignment will create easier and less constricted breathing.

Finally, practice deep, centered breathing. Here are two exercises you can do to free your breath.

Exercise 1

Close your eyes. Take a quick scan of how relaxed you are and where you feel your breath in your body. Now think of one of your favorite flowers, something that has a strong scent. Imagine that this flower is there in front of you. Take in as much of the scent as possible each time you inhale. Indulge in it and appreciate it fully. Now notice how this exercise has altered where you feel breath in your body, since it's from a deeper place. See how relaxed you feel. This is the way you want to breathe.

Exercise 2

Breathe shallowly. Hold your chest up high and take in just a small bit of breath. Now breathe around your rib cage area. Place the palms of your hands on the sides of your rib cage and try not to let your shoulders rise up. Now take deep breaths and enlarge the space by allowing your hands to separate more. Finish by breathing deeply into your belly.

The more you practice such exercises, the more deep breathing will become second nature to you. You will then have a better supply of breath when you are in front of an audience.

Warm-Ups

It's important to find your breath *before you speak.* If you have the right situation, do exercises like deep knee bends or jumping jacks. Our instructors sometimes ask the women in our courses to do these exercises, because they provide the breath of life—and with it energy, vitality, even charisma.

While waiting to give your talk, you can use the smelling exercise to get in touch with your breath. Imagine your favorite flower, or a scent of a spice that you like, and take in that special scent with deep breaths. Nobody needs to know you are in a virtual garden or immersed in a collection of spices! Breathe deeply until it's your turn to speak.

It takes a steady reliable supply of breath to speak powerfully, because the voice without breath has no fuel or power. When your breath strikes your vocal cords and makes them vibrate, you'll get a strong, confident sound—one that mirrors your leadership.

Advice for Leaders of Women

The voice is a powerful instrument of leadership. Members of your team need strong voices to reach their audiences. Women have particular challenges in this area.

- Truly listen to the voices of your team members, especially women.
- Ask yourself: "Do they project the leadership qualities I would like to see in my leaders?" "Do I hear confidence, strength, warmth, energy, and expressiveness?"
- Consult the "Advice for Leaders of Women" sections at the end of chapters 16–20 for ideas on how you can help women project these leadership qualities in their voices.

Chapter Sixteen

Find Your Full Sound

A young woman named Brenda who attended one of our seminars headed home excited that she had learned how to unlock the power of her voice. She told her husband about an exercise she had participated in, in which everyone was asked to stand tall, breathe deeply, and say their names with clarity, power, and a strong intention. While Brenda was demonstrating the techniques, her six-year-old twin daughters were in the background taking it all in. Suddenly they stood before Brenda and her husband, and these two young girls began saying their names loudly and clearly!

"I have never heard them speak with such power," Brenda said, "owning their names with such pleasure and force."

Smiling proudly, she said to her husband, *"This is the voice we want them to keep."*

Not all girls are encouraged to speak with vocal power. Indeed, a woman in our seminar confessed, "I have a three-year-old daughter, Jasmine, who talks very loudly. She's very confident. And I find myself always saying, *Shhhh*—talk quietly. Now I realize I'm setting her up for failure." Many factors contribute to our voices' development as we grow; but if we are to speak as strong, confident leaders, we must discover how to use the full power of our voices.

Surrendering Vocal Power

Do women have strong voices? Absolutely! When we cheer at a sports event, call our families to dinner, or catch a glimpse of a friend across the street and shout, "Let's do lunch, it's been too long!" we have glorious voices. We reach down and find our breath and it vibrates against our vocal chords and we achieve vocal power as a result. So if you expect people to sit up and listen to you at a meeting, you need to engage the same muscles you use when you call to a friend.

But too often women become quieter in the boardroom. We raise our hands and say "Excuse me," but often no one hears us. We're reluctant to use our full sound. Indeed many women have come to think of their voice as something much softer than it really is. When we coach women in our seminars, we ask them to say to their audience, "Am I loud enough?"

"NO!" comes the reply.

"Is that loud enough?"

"NO!"

"IS THAT LOUD ENOUGH?"

"YES."

We have them seek this feedback because they usually hear a level of loudness that's entirely different from what the audience hears. To help them understand this variance, our instructor engages participants in another exercise: she asks each woman to count from 1 to 5 and increase her volume as she does so. Each participant becomes quite loud by the end of the exercise, and our instructor asks the audience what number is most comfortable for listening. Typically, it's 5—and most participants are shocked because it is not their normal speaking volume. They speak in much softer voices that are closer to level 1, because they've convinced themselves that soft is really loud.

There are many reasons we soften our voices, beginning with our early upbringing. The word *shhhh* is a good start in programming us to be quiet. Mothers are often a source of vocal softening. Dora, a participant in one of our seminars, was a very well-put-together woman in her fifties who had recently joined the city council and wanted to find her voice. She spoke in a breathy, barely audible tone. When she was asked to speak five and then ten times louder, she sounded more confident, experienced, and mature. But she stopped and said, "Oh, I must sound bossy. I can hear my mother. She wouldn't be pleased. She'd say I was being bossy." At this point, Dora's daughter, Kathy, who was also in the seminar, piped up, "Mom, don't you think it's time to stop letting Gran run your life?" Dora looked heavenward and speaking to her deceased mother said, "Sorry, Mother, but this is who I really am."

We are further encouraged to speak softly in our careers. As one woman confided, "My boss told me that if I spoke in a higher, quieter voice, I would be more likely to be promoted in this company." As well, today's open office space has encouraged us all—men *and* women—to grow quieter as the workplace walls come down. You might spend hours at your desk keeping your voice down so as not to disturb those around you. It's hard to make the shift from using your "quiet" voice when you enter a boardroom or take part in a conference call. In fact, you might be taking the conference call from your cubicle.

A final source of vocal softening comes from our own inner voices. Women are often reluctant to say anything that will offend. So we frequently deliver tough or strong messages with a quiet, subdued voice—hoping others will either not hear or will respond more positively because of the softness in our voice. One woman said she used to begin messages to her staff with the words "If you don't mind, I'd like you to . . ." and her voice would be soft and apologetic. Now, she says, "I am much more assertive."

All these realities drain our vocal power and lead us to believe that our true voice is a quieter version of the real thing. Unfortunately, "quiet" does not work for leaders. If people have to struggle to hear you, they will tune you out—and likely dismiss you for sounding so powerless. *They will equate a weak voice with weak leadership.* You want to be heard—so you want to have access to vocal strength.

Regaining Your Full Vocal Power

There are several ways you can repossess your rightful sound and develop your full vocal power—from adopting a new mindset to practicing the exercises below.

The starting point is to develop a strong *intention to be heard*. Tell yourself that you have a *right* to be heard, because volume is ultimately about intention. If you resolve to have people hear you clearly and easily, you will strengthen your voice. Successful women and men know this and make a conscious choice to be heard. Joan, an investment banker, told me, "I work with a bunch of men, so I know we women have to talk louder and with more authority. Talking in your 'girl talk' voice just doesn't resonate with them. So I say to myself, 'Okay, I have to speak up without yelling and without annoying the guy sitting right beside me, as opposed to talking down into my paper.'"

If you have a strong intention, you won't let anything get in your way. Cindy, a logistics manager, said, "I had to speak to a group of executives on behalf of our department, which became really hard when the ice maker next to the boardroom suddenly started going, and everything that could go wrong did go wrong. We were near a construction site and a fire truck raced down the street as I was talking. At first I could not speak over the noise, but *I found my voice* with the right volume and was able to deliver my remarks without focusing on whether I was talking loudly. I just did it."

Be careful not to become shrill when you add volume. Sometimes women increase their pitch and sound aggressive or shrill when they begin to speak louder. A participant in our program explained, "In general I am loud, and speak with energy behind it—but I discovered that as I get louder the pitch of my voice becomes shocking. I sound unsure of myself at that high pitch." She is not alone. Former British prime minister Margaret Thatcher had a problem with a high-pitched voice. As she put it, "One has to speak over the din to get a hearing in the House of Commons. This is more difficult the higher the pitch of one's voice, because in increasing its volume one automatically goes up the register. This poses an obvious problem for most women. Somehow one has to learn to project the voice without shrieking."[1] Thatcher took voice lessons and lowered her voice and sounded more sympathetic,[2] which is something you might consider doing if you feel you sound aggressive or shrill when you use your full voice. Record yourself to see whether your pitch is too high; self-correct or take some voice coaching.

Still another important step toward achieving vocal power is *accepting* your more powerful voice. Some people will tell you not to change your voice; friends, colleagues, husbands, and bosses may like it the way it is.

This new level of volume can be threatening, even scary. We observed two men in one of our seminars who had a friendly relationship with one of the women. They rushed to her defense when our instructor suggested she could be vocally stronger, and said, "Oh, you don't know Jessica. She walks into a room and she gets a lot of respect." "Well," our instructor said, "you know her and have worked with her for twelve years. You are like her big brothers. You're saying, 'Don't push Jessica. We like her the way she is.' But what if she wants to be promoted? What if she has to prove herself to strangers? She'll need a stronger voice." At this point, Jessica stepped in to thank her colleagues for their advice—and proclaimed, "I would like to develop my voice so others hear confidence and respect me because of it."

Finally, you need to *practice* to achieve your complete vocal power. You already have great equipment; you just need to use it fully and regularly to retain that strength. The following exercises will enable you to discover your voice's authority. If you want to audibly convey the leader you are, commit to letting the vibrations resonate through your body whenever you speak. Commit fully to having your ideas heard when you're speaking in a meeting, on the phone, or at the front of a large room. Come into your own full sound, and know that you can be assertive without losing your grace. Take a deep breath and truly speak up.

Exercise 1: Singing

You can develop the habit of turning up your volume by getting comfortable with the sound of your voice through singing. If you're shy about singing in front of others, the shower is one place you're alone and don't have to worry about others listening. It works really well too—the hot water relaxes you, and the acoustics are great so you gain the confidence to sing even louder. Sing along with your favorite artists in your car. Get used to the sound and feeling of vibrations moving through your body. Once you become accustomed to the sound of your own voice, you will become addicted to the idea of hearing yourself.

Exercise 2: Yawning

Actor Morgan Freeman—who is recognized for his distinctive voice—advises, "If you're looking to improve the sound of your voice, yawn a lot. It relaxes your throat muscles, relaxes your vocal cords, and as soon as they relax, the tone drops."[3]

Exercise 3: Finding Your Sound

Imagine you have just come to the end of a long day or journey and are finally sitting in a place that gives you relief or peace. Tune into that sense of relief, breathe in deeply, and release the air with a big sigh. Do so again. Now take that big sigh and see if you can add sound to it. Instead of just releasing air, there's now a sound that accompanies it. We recognize that sound—the sigh of relief. Let it go. At the end of one of those delicious voiced sighs, close your lips and end the sigh with a hum. Try it again. Elongate that hum, and try and set up a vibration in the lips. This exercise connects breath and sound.

Practice these exercises, and others will regard you as a leader who truly speaks up.

Advice for Leaders of Women

Volume can be an issue for both male and female leaders. Women can sometimes sound loud or have high-pitched tones, but more commonly they speak too softly and in so doing, sound tentative or lacking in confidence.

- If you believe a woman on your team needs to develop a stronger voice, mention this to her.
- Ask her if she is aware she sounds "soft" or "low keyed" and is difficult to hear or if she is aware she sounds less confident than she could.

- Suggest a number of steps she can take, such as (1) listening to herself on a voice recorder; (2) rehearsing her presentations out loud, paying attention to the sound of her voice; (3) adjusting her voice for a better volume during meetings.
- Practice with her or support her in working with a voice coach.
- If she is too loud, urge her to adopt a more conversational tone.

Chapter Seventeen

Develop Your Leader's Voice

B arbara is in her late twenties and speaks with a relentlessly cheerful voice that can get on people's nerves. She is always smiling, happy, and eager—and sounds as though she's ten years younger than she really is. During the training session, our instructor asks her whether she ever uses a different voice.

"Oh no, I speak like this all the time!"

Barbara is beginning to suspect that her voice and her chipperness may be an issue. The instructor asks her whether she used another voice during any time in her life. At first, she replies, "Oh, no; this is the way I've always spoken." Then upon reflection, she blurts out.

"Oh my goodness—I remember now! I used to have a completely different voice when I was head of my debating society at university!"

Our instructor prods, "What was your voice like back then?"

"It was way, way lower. People would say I was one of the best debaters they'd heard."

"So what happened?" our instructor asked.

"I don't know." (Barbara thinks for a few seconds.) "Oh yes, I do. It's my boss. I'm not blaming him or anything; he's a good boss. It's just that ever since I started working with him—six years ago when I was straight out of university—he's asked me to smile. Every morning during those first few months I reported to him, he'd walk up to my desk and say, 'Where's that smile?' Sometimes he'd say it twice or three times in one day."

She continues, "It's just his way. He has three daughters, so that's how he likes to relate to me—like I'm one of his daughters. I know he's not comfortable around some of the stronger women in the office. So smiling makes us more agreeable to him."

"Do you see how this could have interfered with your career?" our instructor asks.

Barbara nods slowly. This story hangs in the air for a bit as each participant contemplates her own history. For the rest of the two-day workshop Barbara is not smiling continuously. She seems to be coming from a different place in herself. Her voice is far more relaxed and starting to drop down into her lower registers. During one improvisation when Barbara has to hold her own in a discussion on policy, we see the brilliant debater start to reemerge. She is determined from now on not to give up her authentic voice—even if that means she has to leave her boss, which she suspects she will have to do.

This story says a lot about our voice—and how it is shaped by external realities. Finding your true leadership voice often requires a journey like Barbara's—one of self-discovery and commitment to change.

Our Many Voices

Our voice is developed from very real life experiences—and the sound we acquire from these experiences becomes part of our identity. But we need to assess how we sound as we move into leadership roles. We need to ask, "Do I sound like a leader? Do I have a voice that people would want to listen to and follow?" If your answer is "no" or you are not sure, you will likely want to make a change. Voices like the following can undermine female leaders by making them sound less confident than they need to be.

- *The little girl voice.* This high-pitched, thin, and wispy tone makes the speaker sound younger and less confident than she really is. It lacks the depth of a woman who sounds like a leader. One VP we worked with was petite and young looking, so she thought her little girl voice served her very well. Then she realized that her voice had not evolved with her age and with her executive position.

- *The cheerleader voice.* This makes the speaker sound weak because she is trying so hard. After all, if you don't think people will listen to you, you're going to try even harder. This frequently happens when a woman gets passionate about a topic and seeks buy-in. The cheerleader pulls out all the stops, pushes her voice into the higher registers, picks up her pace, smiles a lot, and uses lots of "fly-away" energy. This voice lacks the gravitas and grounded commitment of a leader.

- *The maternal voice.* This voice can be either loud and controlling or quietly domineering. A client came to us for coaching because she whispered when she spoke. She traced it back to the fact that she'd worked as a kindergarten teacher and had learned to get children's attention with a quiet maternal voice. The problem was that people had to lean in to hear her speak, and her voice sounded and felt manipulative.

- *The helpful voice.* This voice positions the speaker as a subordinate. A woman in one of our courses had a wealth of experience and smarts, and was the sort of woman who could probably run a company. But her voice made her sound much lower in rank than she was. It turned out that she had begun her work life in a secretarial position; her voice got "stuck" in that role and never matured.

- *The girlfriend voice.* This is a sweet, coy voice that may get attention in the office, but for the wrong reasons. It's the vocal equivalent of short skirts and cleavage. It may have its side benefits, but it doesn't work for someone who is career focused. This is not uncommon even among women who have no hidden agendas.

- *The nice voice.* This is one of the more common voices women use; unfortunately, "nice" lacks power. In fact, being nice in the board room conveys the impression that you are trying to make others feel good—thereby putting *them* in the power position and belittling your leadership.

- *The grateful voice.* This tone can suggest that a woman feels she doesn't deserve to be heard. One woman explained, "That gratefulness suggests we are not comfortable being at the table, and indicates we're not as invested in the issues as other participants present."

- *The manly voice*. This is less common today than it once was, when women took on the male style to fit into a male-dominated work environment. This voice is low, often aggressive, and shows little or no warmth. In the movie *The Devil Wears Prada*, Meryl Streep plays an executive who adopts those tones.

If you identify with one of these voices, consider whether it serves you well as a leader. These voices play to a different audience and reflect a different time or role in our lives. It's important to leave them behind if you want to sound like a leader. Once you abandon them, you will be able to open yourself up to your leadership voice.

When we asked a woman with the helpful voice if she had another voice, she replied without skipping a beat: "Do you mean like this?" in a deep, commanding pitch. "This is the voice I use to call my kids. They know I mean business!" She was comfortable leading in her role as a mother. We need to reclaim those stronger voices if we want to sound like authentic leaders.

Your Authentic Leadership Voice

So how do you go about developing your leader's voice?

Begin by finding the courage to abandon any of the less effective voices discussed in this chapter and getting in touch with your own authentic leadership tone. And it *does* take courage. You're changing the *way you sound* and developing a stronger vocal identity. I remember back in 2003 when one woman in a seminar spoke up and proudly announced, "Since the last session, I've adopted a more confident tone. I don't sound anymore like I am sitting there waiting to do whatever people give me to do." She added, "It's tough. I have to keep reminding myself that I don't have to sound obliging all the time. But it's fun seeing people reacting to the new me."

Developing your authentic leader's voice also involves speaking with the same warmth and energy you use in everyday conversation. If you want people to hear you as approachable and passionate, then practice finding those same qualities in your voice. If you want board members to recognize that you're determined and excited about an idea, make sure you convey those feelings in your voice. Speaking with that natural expressiveness is critical for a leader.

Your leader's voice will also be natural and energetic if you speak with your own words. A woman in our seminar, whose job was to sell retail space in shopping malls, was vibrant during the break, telling other participants who had gathered around her about the huge shopping mall in the lower level of the building they were in and how it was connected to miles and miles of other shopping malls. All her listeners were enthralled. But when she got up to give her presentation, her language became stilted; the "shopping mall" suddenly became a "retail center" and the miles and miles of shops became "square footage" and "leased space." Unsurprisingly, her voice lost its animation and its audience! But once she reclaimed her own vocabulary, her presentation became more akin to the informal narrative she had delivered during the break, and her audience once again became captivated. If you want to be a leader, your voice must be true to the way you normally speak, and that means using your own words!

Having an authentic leader's voice means speaking with conviction. Don't just say what you think others want to hear; this can be a trap for women who wish to please. You must articulate your convictions. The greatest historical and corporate leaders are those who have given voice to what they believe. They stand for something, and we know what they stand for!

Developing an authentic leader's voice involves still another quality: *gravitas*. Recently I coached a vice president of a hedge fund. She was the only female on the executive team, and she asked me to consult with the managing partner to see how she might improve her speaking style. He praised her in many areas, but said, "Elizabeth needs more gravitas. She will be in meetings with money managers and will have to help convince them to commit millions of dollars to us. She needs to sound credible." *Gravitas* literally means to be "grounded." It is a quality I hear senior executives mention frequently with respect to what leaders— particularly female leaders—need.

Gravitas has several dimensions. To begin with, it involves your tone— your deeper, stronger voice that conveys seriousness. It would be impossible to project gravitas if you have a high, squeaky voice, or a voice that's prettied up or too nice. Another aspect of gravitas is having "substance," "weight," and "dignity." People with gravitas are taken seriously because they speak with weight and substance and their audience knows that they are saying something important. Still another dimension of gravitas is having a track record that underlies what you say. You not only have to be grounded in terms of your tone and substance; you have to be credible as someone who practices what she preaches.

Having an authentic leadership voice involves outgrowing other voices that don't work for you as a leader, and being genuine, having conviction, and showing gravitas by grounding yourself in tone, substance, and accomplishment. This is a voice that people will listen to and one that will lead them.

Advice for Leaders of Women

Make sure your leaders *sound* like leaders. Women can get stuck in vocal patterns that do not represent them as leaders. For example, they may sound youthful, cheerleaderish, maternal, teacherly, too nice, or helpful. They may not even be aware that they are projecting this kind of tone. You can help them.

- Be sure not to encourage or reinforce such vocal patterns.
- If you hear a woman on your team speaking with such a voice, take her aside and help her understand the gap between how she sounds and how a leader should sound. You might say, for example, "Sounding so cheerful can get in the way of sounding like a leader."
- If the problem persists, support her with coaching.

Chapter Eighteen

Pace Yourself

D anielle is a delightful conversationalist. But when she speaks to a group of more than a few people, she talks so fast that her audience feels lost in some frantic race. She runs her words together. She snatches at breaths. It's both unsettling to watch her and difficult to grasp what she's saying. When our instructor asks her to slow down, she laughs; it's not the first time she's heard this. She slows down for about eight seconds, and then she's off again at a breakneck pace. When she is reminded again to slow down, she does so—but again, only briefly. Yet it *is* long enough for the instructor and participants to recognize an appreciable difference in her delivery and effectiveness—to hear her words and grasp their meaning.

There is at least one woman in every Taking the Stage seminar who races through her speech at lightning speed. Many others accelerate their pace when delivering their remarks. And it's not simply a matter of changing the mechanics by slowing down. As you can see from Danielle's example, people often revert to speaking fast even when they're encouraged to take their time. Pace reflects a larger issue: *one's relationship to an audience*. And the solution lies in owning the room and pacing yourself so you can engage the people listening to you.

Why We Talk Too Fast

Talking fast is not reserved for women alone. There are reasons both genders accelerate their pace. "Type A" or nervous speakers have a tendency to speak fast. People also race when they feel (mistakenly) that they need to pile on the information, or when they're rushing to get to the next meeting. They also speed up when their time is reduced and they must compress their talks. Fast talking may also be shaped by the rapid-fire communications inherent in new technology. But along with these reasons, many women speak too fast because they don't feel they can hold the room.

Women often pick up their pace because they are afraid of being interrupted—and for good reason! Men are far more likely to interrupt women than women are to interrupt men—as was shown in chapter 8. Speeding up gives women some small feeling of being in control. As one woman wrote, "It's OK when I talk and don't pause; nobody will interrupt me if I keep talking." But this is not real control. It is reactive behavior based on fear. The faster delivery also makes them less effective in reaching their audience.

Some women speak fast because they are uncomfortable in the spotlight. We hear from women that they "want to get it over quickly," they "hate to impose themselves" and "don't want to take up the audience's time." As one participant said, "You just want to get it done and out of the way." These women are not convinced they deserve to have the floor.

Still other women may accelerate their pace because they don't feel the audience is listening. This can be true of any situation, but particularly with conference calls, where they can't see the audience so are more likely to make negative assumptions about their attention—or lack thereof. One woman told me she was frustrated during an important conference call. "It was difficult to reach people, because seven were in Las Vegas eating lunch, one was in Florida, and three were with me in Montreal. Side conversations were happening remotely. It was a real challenge!" She was so distracted thinking about who *wasn't* paying attention that she rushed through her talk. A man would have likely assumed his remarks were important and that everyone was listening. He might even have engaged them in the discussion to make sure they *were* listening.

We've also observed that some women rush to the end of their remarks because they lack confidence that they can sell their ideas to their audience. This involves either "jumping to the conclusion," as one woman put it, or giving over the presentation to discussion before finishing—because as another said, "I assumed that I was not going to be able to convince the people about what I needed to get done."

Women often surrender power in all these situations. Their uncomfortable relationship with their audience leads them to pick up their pace and relinquish the opportunity to sway their audience. Their listeners see someone who might appear frazzled, hard to understand, and not committed to the messages they are delivering.

Owning the Room

The solution is to first accept your right to be heard and then adopt a more deliberate pace to convey your message. I call this right to be heard "owning the room." If you can embrace that mindset, you'll have the audience waiting for each word you deliver. Great leaders have this rapport with their audiences; they control the conversation's content, timing, and tone. Listen to a typical TED talk, and you'll see speakers who own the room.

You can achieve this perspective by telling yourself that you deserve the audience's attention because you've prepared well and your topic is important for them. Think positively about your virtual audience during conference calls. Assume they will pay attention, and focus on your own presentation and what you have to say, rather than whether they are eating their lunch or texting others. Once you feel in touch with your audience, take control by slowing your pace. You can do this in many ways.

First, pause to collect your thoughts *before* speaking. Once you adopt a positive mindset and feel confident that people will listen, you will be more likely to take the time to collect your thoughts. And you'll be more credible if you're not scrambling for ideas while speaking.

Second, speak in a slow, conversational pace. Don't rush the words. We speak more slowly in conversation because we want that one important listener to stay with us. Think of how you talk at home, with friends, or in the cafeteria with your colleagues; that's the pace you should adopt when you speak in front of an audience. Your listeners will be more likely to stay with you if you talk to them with a relaxed, conversational pace. And you will sound more confident.

Third, use pauses when you speak. My first business partner, Marshall Bell, an actor, had a wonderful expression: "No pause is ever too long." Pauses make you sound supremely confident, and they enable your audience to process what you have just said. Think about it: an audience absorbs what you've said *after* you have said it . . . *during* the pauses. While you are delivering an idea, they hear it only with their *ears*. But after, they hear it with their *minds*. Pausing after each sentence will enable your audience to mentally process your ideas.

How long should you pause between sentences? A rough estimate is two seconds (the time it takes to slowly say, "one potato, two potato"). When you are anxious, that two-second pause may feel like twenty minutes. But don't rush it. It's a mark of good speaking (and leadership) that you give your audience those pauses so they can reflect on what you've said. The pause has an additional benefit for you: it enables you to breathe and think through your next thought.

Longer pauses should follow your key ideas—your message, main proof points, call to action, and any other defining statements. Indeed, they can also be cues that you've completed a paragraph. As well, pausing before your message or any other key statement tells the audience, "Listen: I have something important to say." So practice the pauses. And if you maintain a grounded voice and strong eye contact, you will hold the room.

Fourth, *vary* your pace. We don't speak with a uniform pace. We tend to naturally slow down for more important statements and pick up our pace for less important ones. For example, a manager might say, "I am confident we can deliver this project on time and on budget" with a slow pace to bring emphasis to her idea. But to elaborate on this statement, that same speaker will pick up her pace and say (as though delivering a list), "The team has been working hard on this project. They are very capable and committed. They've kept to the timetable. They are working overtime when they need to, and they have closely monitored the costs." There is a nice rhythm to that. So deliver your key statements with a slower pace and present supporting statements with a quickened pace.

This variation in pace will keep your audience more engaged, and it will alert them to what's important and what's secondary.

Fifth, use your full, allotted time. You deserve it! If you have thirty minutes, take twenty to deliver the presentation, and ten for Q&A. Take time to bring your audience through your entire thought process, and don't get derailed by anyone looking at their watch. *Own the opportunity* to sell your idea and complete the proof points. Don't give up the floor before you are finished. This can be a challenge, particularly if you are speaking to busy senior executives. As tempting as it can be, don't rush through the entire presentation fast and furiously if they say, "I only have five minutes." Instead, deliver the "bones" of your talk. You can forego the detail, but remember the power of pauses. This approach will allow you to complete a brief presentation without rushing.

Pace is critical to your success as a leader. Speaking at the proper clip makes clear your conviction that you have a right to be heard, and that you're presenting valuable information. Take ownership of your communications by using a natural, relaxed, and easy pace for the audience to follow. This will also allow you to be expressive and use the techniques discussed in the remaining chapters of the book.

Advice for Leaders of Women

Women tend to speak faster than men in business settings when they think they may be interrupted or fear others may not be taking them seriously. You can help them.

- When chairing a meeting, be approachable and use active listening skills to create an inclusive atmosphere. This will reduce stress and, in turn, minimize their need to rush.
- If someone is speaking too quickly—and the messaging is blurred— stop that individual and say, "Can you take us through that once again . . . more slowly?"
- If a women typically speaks fast, or in a rushed manner, have a coaching conversation and find out what the issue is and help her find a solution.

Chapter Nineteen

Be Expressive

Not long ago, I interviewed a young woman for an internship at The Humphrey Group. She had good credentials on paper: she was a university undergraduate with high grades and had excelled in extra-curricular activities. But within minutes of meeting her, I knew that I would not bring her in. She used lots of "um's," "you know's," and other filler words; but most grating was her *upspeak*. She lifted her voice at the end of *every sentence* as though asking a question. Repeated patterns like this can drive listeners crazy.

We do a disservice to ourselves when we use our voices in such unexpressive ways. Our vocal chords—and all the parts of our upper body from our chest and lungs to our throat and mouth—make up a remarkably expressive instrument. We can cover a range of two-and-a-half octaves. That's *do, re, mi, fa, so, la, ti, do*, more than twice over. But we often limit ourselves to a small portion of this range—less than one octave. And the "music" we create within this narrow bandwidth of sound does not support our ideas. This chapter shows how using our voices expressively draws people to us and adds excitement to our ideas. It is critical to use all our notes to reinforce the substance of our remarks.

Down with Upspeak

One way we limit our expressiveness is by using *upspeak*, as the young woman in the opening story did. This has become an unfortunate vocal epidemic among women—and has even spread to some men. Lifting the voice at the end of sentences—turning statements into questions—not only grates on the ears; it also makes the speaker sound young and unsure of herself. If you want to know what it sounds like, read aloud the following passage—from a woman to her boss:

> *I'm working on the report? Will have it to you by tomorrow? I hope you like it?*

The question marks mimic upspeak and show how tentative it sounds. Why do many women use it? In part, it's because they seek reinforcement from their audience. As one woman told me, "My habit of lifting my voice at the end of sentences is a substitute for 'Okay?' which I used to say at the end of each thought." Upspeak adds a note of pleading by asking, "Do you agree?" or "Should I go on?" Some women fall into this pattern of speech because they think it makes them more approachable. A recent *New York Times* article described how a journalist regularly used upspeak because, as she stated, it "may cause a source to open up to me." [1] Still, she went to a speech coach because people on the phone regularly asked her, "How old are you?" Upspeak makes you sound less certain, less confident, less mature—less like a leader. So don't even think about using it! And if you do have this pattern in your voice, become conscious of it, and ground yourself in each sentence when you speak. Don't "lift off" at the end of sentences. You *can* get beyond it.

Mind Your Monotone

Another vocal pattern that limits our expressiveness is speaking in a monotone voice. Both men and women can fall into the habit of using this limited vocal bandwidth. This pattern often reflects a lack of connection to what we are saying, a lack of conviction. Indeed, when we speak with so few notes listeners think we aren't fully committed to our message or our topic. A monotone voice can also be the result of speaking to an electronic medium rather than to a person—so in our voicemail messages we often flatten out our expression and lose our warmth. The result can be to convey less of a connection to people than we'd like.

For women, a monotone voice can also signal a fear of sounding too strong or too expressive—a reluctance to take the stage and put ourselves out there. Monotone is a safe haven for those who fear that the audience may not agree with them.

Although there are various reasons why people adopt this limited range, using a single note or very few notes never sends a positive message. You will not energize an audience with a monotone. People may even stop listening to you. Listen to yourself, and if you hear yourself speaking in a lackluster way, work on being more expressive.

Don't Get Stuck in the Upper Registers

Still another way women limit their expressiveness is getting stuck in the upper vocal registers. We hear this in some of the women we coach, and the result is that they sound unlike the leaders they are. The sound waves initiated by the vocal cords resonate wherever they are permitted to—in our chest, our throat, our mouth and nose, even in the bones of our face and head. Sometimes we allow those sound waves to vibrate only in our heads—high up—so we develop a little girl or a cheerleader voice. If you always sound youthfully cheerful and obliging, the audience will not recognize your maturity, experience, and ability to lead.

Some women send their voices into their noses because of habit or tension, and they sound whiney or nagging. These tones, too, do not represent leadership. One of our instructors told a story of overhearing a conversation between a male boss and a female employee in an elevator. It was the end of summer and the boss asked, "So what did you do on your summer vacation?" The female employee hunched her shoulders and retreated right into her nose, and said, "Oh, nothing very interesting." Here was an opportunity to reveal something of herself to a boss who only knew her at work. She could have said, "I sat on the dock each night and saw the most exquisite sunsets for two weeks; it was all so relaxing, and now I'm ready to get back to work." Instead, she conveyed the message, "I'm boring so leave me alone." What bothered our instructor most was that the woman seemed *proud* of being boring—because it got her off the hook. Vocally, her nose seemed to be her safest place.

This kind of nasality can be an unconscious pattern developed by someone who was bullied as a child and still goes around with a sound that says, "Leave me alone," or "I'm weak, so I am going to hide." But none of these upper-register voices—whether the high, squeaky, little girl voice or the whiney nasal voice—works for a leader.

Instead of getting stuck in your upper registers, find a way to pitch your voice lower so it comes not only from your upper registers but also from your throat and chest. These notes bring weight and maturity to a voice. You'll want to practice developing them because they give you a more grounded sound. Men use these lower notes more frequently than women do, sometimes by tucking their chins in and pushing their voices down to sound manly. But if they leave out the higher registers, they too limit their voices and lose a great deal of expression.

How can you access these lower registers? Actress Lauren Bacall tells how she developed her deep, sultry voice. "It was [movie director Howard] Hawks' advice," she said, "to keep my voice low even when I was excited. So I practiced by reading *The Robe* aloud sitting in my car. I didn't just suddenly get a low voice."[2] How do audiences react to Bacall's voice—and how would they react to your developing a deeper, more independent voice? According to Bacall, "It gives people the impression that I'm formidable, when I'm really quite vulnerable."[3] Those deeper registers will give your voice a quality that suggests you are strong, formidable, and leader-like.

Margaret Thatcher also worked with a coach from the National Theatre. According to Max Atkinson, author of *Our Masters' Voices: The Language and Body Language of Politics*, she successfully lowered her voice "almost half the average difference in pitch between male and female voices."[4] By changing her voice, too, she also slowed down her speech, which according to Atkinson is a natural result of lowering the voice's pitch.[5]

Vary Your Sound

Women (and men) can lose their expressiveness when they use the same few notes or repeat the same pattern over and over. You can practice being more expressive in a variety of ways. Let me suggest several.

In meetings, ask yourself, "When I make a point, does my voice engage others with its expressiveness?" If you are not reaching people, try modulating your voice more. Watch their response as you do so. Or, target the one person in the room who is not listening, and see if varying your sound will bring him or her around.

In voicemails, listen to what you have recorded, and if it sounds flat, rerecord it until it captures your true voice. Also listen to your outgoing messages before you push SEND. If needed, rerecord them to make them more expressive.

For speeches and presentations, rehearse yourself or get some good professional coaching. You can even practice with a family member or colleague. I once had a client who rehearsed with her young son. She would read her speech aloud, and he would stop her regularly to say "Mom, that doesn't sound like you." Children know—and let us know—when we're not being real. Marking up your text with "expression marks" can also be incredibly helpful. These are annotations that indicate where to pause and what words to emphasize. I've included a portion of the text I delivered when I received an Entrepreneur of the Year Award. The double slashes are pause marks and the underlines are for emphasis. (Try reading it!)

> It took // <u>courage</u> to <u>start</u> my business. It took // <u>courage</u> to <u>face</u> my early balance sheets. //// It also took <u>courage</u> of a deeper sort to <u>envision</u> what the business could become. Waking up each morning and <u>reinventing</u> the business. It's a never-ending creation. You can never let it go. The business is always with you. It becomes part of your // <u>soul.</u>

The high-impact words are underlined and must be delivered with a stronger tone and slower pace. Key words also have slashes before them, indicating a slight pause that creates a sense of anticipation.

In summary, develop your expressiveness to become a more engaging speaker. Eliminate upspeak, avoid a monotone delivery, don't confine yourself to the higher registers, and vary your sound. People will be more likely to listen to you. Here are a few exercises to help you achieve that fuller vocal range.

Exercise 1: Give Up Upspeak

The best way to eliminate upspeak is to ask a trusted colleague or mentor to listen and tell you whether it sounds as though you are asking a question when you really aren't. You can also record yourself and listen to the playback. Practice again, and listen to the improvement.

Exercise 2: Beyond Monotone

Read a passage from an author you enjoy or a children's book and let your voice move up and down the scale. Exaggerate the expression. Start sentences on new notes. (Remember, when we start each sentence on the same note, we can easily fall into a monotone delivery.) Another way of moving beyond monotone: listen to readings by actors for the range of notes they use, and do your best to copy that expressiveness.

Exercise 3: Lower Your Pitch

One approach, Lauren Bacall's, is to go to a place where no one will hear you (hers was a car parked on a deserted spot above Beverly Hills), and read a passage or an entire book with a lower voice. And do this every day, as she did. Alternatively, hire a speech coach, as Margaret Thatcher did, and you will learn to lower your voice through humming and other exercises.

Exercise 4: Finding All Your Notes

To discover what a remarkable vocal instrument you have, try these different ways of making sounds:

- Hum deeply into your chest and put your hand there to feel the vibrations.
- Next, hum on a slightly higher note and feel the vibrations in your throat, face, and nose. See how the top of your head vibrates with a still higher note.
- Hum into your mouth resonator with your lips only slightly parted and your jaw held tight and closed. Then release that tension by

(continued)

(*continued*)

   massaging your jaw hinge with the heels of your hands and yawn.
   Try that same sound again.
- Now open your mouth wide and blow into your hand—and then
  let out a large sigh. Listen to how much stronger your voice is
  when you open your mouth wide, relax your jaw muscles, and
  release the vibrations from inside your mouth.

In sum, make full use of the powerful vocal instrument each of us
possesses. Practice using the full range of notes. And let your vocal
music fully reinforce the messages you deliver.

Advice for Leaders of Women

Men and women can both learn to be more expressive. Here's how you can
help people express themselves more effectively.

- If you hear a woman lifting her voice at the end of sentences—in a
  pattern called upspeak—mention it to her. This habit of sounding
  like she's asking a question when she's really not makes her sound
  tentative.
- If you hear a woman speaking in a monotone voice, mention it. Say
  "You may want to work on your vocal presence. I find sometimes your
  voice doesn't carry the expression I know you feel."
- If a woman speaks in a high-pitched voice, take a leaf out of movie
  director Howard Hawks's book. He encouraged Lauren Bacall to lower
  her voice, and she sounded much more grounded and confident.

Chapter Twenty

Articulate Clearly

I n the musical *My Fair Lady*, Eliza Doolittle is transformed from a cockney flower girl into a British lady, all due to a change in her pronunciation. Her speech coach, Henry Higgins, believed that enunciation was far more important in defining her status than social class or wealth. And he was right! At an embassy party she was accepted as a woman "of royal blood."[1] While none of us wants to pass as royalty in the business world, we do want to portray leadership—and the way we enunciate our words can make a huge difference in how people perceive us. This chapter suggests how you can improve your articulation, and strengthen your center stage voice.

Why A-R-T-I-C-U-L-A-T-E?

We all speak thousands of words every day—but to sound like leaders, we must put commitment and energy into forming our words. As Nicky Guadagni, a senior instructor in our firm, tells our clients, "Your audience has to understand *every word* you are saying. You can't get away with mumbling. If you rush and slur your words or fail to enunciate them clearly, no one will be able to follow you or grasp your brilliant ideas."

The way you pronounce or don't pronounce words can reflect many things. Mumbling through your thoughts can be a way of hiding or withholding yourself in a situation where you don't feel comfortable. It can also be a vestige of our earlier teenage years, when we may have been less forthcoming and didn't necessarily want anyone to hear us. Poor enunciation can also reflect the fact that you're not speaking in your first language and certain sounds in your adopted language are difficult for you. For example, the *th* sound in English is difficult for many people, and some get confused by *w* and *v*.

Finally, weak articulation can come from the fact that we are using an everyday voice for leadership situations. If your words are worth speaking, they are worth delivering clearly. If you don't articulate precisely, an audience may be left feeling that you aren't committed to what you are saying—and will be less likely to heed your call to action or promote you into a new role.

The Art of Articulation

To "articulate" literally means to "break up into bits"[2]—and that is what you do when you form words. You take a stream of sound and break it up into intelligible bits. Our articulators—our tongue and lips—are critical, because you don't want people leaning forward and asking, "What did you say?"

You need to "warm up" your articulators, which we don't do enough. One of the simplest and most effective exercises is to stick your tongue firmly outside your mouth, and practice counting to ten while keeping your tongue outside your mouth. If you are with someone else (hopefully not a first date!), look at that person and try to say, "One, two, three, four" and so forth with your tongue out. You can also practice this exercise with any piece of text for a minute or two. Once you've completed the counting or the text, speak it again with your tongue back inside your mouth. Notice how open your sound is and how easily you articulate.

If you are going into a meeting to present, find an opportunity in a private area—whether driving in your car or in a corridor near the meeting room—to do this same exercise. With your tongue out, deliver your opening: "Good morning. Thank you all for coming to hear about our plans for restructuring our customer accounts." And with your tongue still out, go through the first paragraph of what you are going to say.

Another way to practice articulating is to open your whole jaw and bring muscularity to the formation of your words. The next time you're in a crowded room, perhaps before a big presentation when there are lots of people milling about, give your lips a good workout just trying to be clear above the din—not by shouting, but by committing to articulation. It's the feeling of speaking to someone who is hard of hearing. If you bring that same energy to a presentation or to a conference call, you will sound and feel more deliberate and committed.

I once practiced articulation with one of our coaches, Maggie Huculak, during a round of rehearsals. "I'm in your hands," I said to Maggie. She immediately told me, "Your articulation needs strengthening; your energy is falling off at the end of sentences and at the end of words." (That might have been because I had spent day and night writing fifteen drafts of my speech.) The solution, she told me, was twofold. "Breathe more, so you can drive your thoughts right to the end of each sentence. And within each sentence, commit more fully to the consonants that frame each word." (The consonants are all the letters of the alphabet *except* the vowels *a, e, i, o, u,* and sometimes *y.*) With her guidance, I began delivering my speech aloud, emphasizing each consonant. Try it! You'll find that focusing on the consonants makes each word sound much clearer and more powerful. For example in the word *proud,* make sure the *p* and the *d* are heard. In the word *lead,* bring out the *l* and *d.* Now say "proud to lead" with those consonants coming forward. This focus on articulation also forced me to breathe more and enabled me to sustain each thought to the end of the sentence. Next time you're at a play, listen to how the actors speak with clear consonants.

For daily practice, think of the tongue twisters you learned when you were growing up. Now is the time to revive them and practice them daily. And it doesn't matter what language they're in—they're brilliant exercises for your articulating muscles. Here's a good one to practice. It's from Gilbert and Sullivan's opera, *The Mikado.*

> To sit in solemn silence, in a dull dark dock.
> In a pestilential prison, with a life-long lock.
> Awaiting the sensation, of a short sharp shock.
> From a cheap and chippy chopper, on a big black block.[3]

Now, repeat this passage with your tongue out. Now repeat it with your tongue in.

These exercises should limber up your articulators and wake up their muscles. They will make your speaking sharper, cleaner, and clearer. We talk all day without ever warming up. We begin with an important meeting at nine o'clock in the morning. If we live alone we may not have spoken or used our voice at all. So these warm-ups are really important.

If you suspect you have difficulty pronouncing or delivering words, get help—from a workmate, a friend, or a professional coach. Practice daily and record yourself. When you listen to that recording, don't be overly self-critical. Notice first what you like about your voice. Then observe what you might like to improve on.

Doing all these exercises will enable you to develop your voice as a powerful leadership tool. It is worth your time, because it has a direct impact when you are giving a presentation or simply leaving a voicemail message. You will enjoy speaking even more. As one of our instructors put it, "Articulation simply means 'tasting your words.'"

Advice for Leaders of Women

Leaders of women don't need to transform themselves into Henry Higgins, who helped Eliza Doolittle learn to speak properly in My Fair Lady. But those skills advanced her status, and they can do the same for women in business. Individuals who use their voices well will be stronger assets to your team.

- If there are people on your staff who have difficulty pronouncing their words or who mumble, don't ignore the issue. Talk to them about it.
- Offer to support them with voice coaching. A series of sessions will enable them to get their ideas across more clearly through better articulation.
- Be patient. This change can take time—often months, even years. But with the right motivation and support great progress is possible.

Part Four

Stand Out on Stage

Chapter Twenty-One

Understand the Power of Presence

Imagine a person sitting across from you at a table. At first you don't notice that quiet and self-effacing individual; but when she sits up straight and begins to speak, she becomes present in an utterly compelling way. What has she done? She has turned up a dial within herself, and tapped an inner energy—of courage, and of risk. It is an expansive energy that serves as the foundation of being fully present.

These words from Linda Griffiths, a playwright and instructor in The Humphrey Group, perfectly describe the power of presence—the focus of this book's final section. When you are on stage—whether it's at a podium, in a meeting room, on a conference call, or in a corridor conversation—you want to have a strong physical presence that engages your audience. The following chapters show you how to achieve that by understanding the power of presence, overcoming nervousness, standing and sitting tall, using strong body language, and dressing for your leadership role. Mastering these skills will give you a strong presence. You will stand out on stage.

But what exactly *is* "presence"?

Quite simply, it is the act of being fully present on stage. Just look at the word itself. *Presence* means to be "present." Yet, when a senior executive says about a team member, "I want her to have more 'presence,'" he seems to be talking about something more compelling. Indeed, many senior leaders want to have or want their team members to display more "presence," or "executive presence," or "leadership presence."

Presence can be an elusive quality. Yet we know it immediately when we see it in another person. We say people have a strong presence—a certain magnetism—when they are centered and draw us to them. Think of the female leaders on the world stage who impress you. Facebook COO Sheryl Sandberg is a business leader who has inspired the world with her book, *Lean In.*[1] If you see her speak, you'll find she is equally inspiring because she has presence.[2] She clearly is deeply committed to the thoughts she shares. She conveys a warm, generous, authentic energy. Hillary Clinton has a different kind of presence—more determined and driven. We expect that from a woman who has reached the pinnacle of political power. And Malala Yousafzai, the young Pakistani crusader for women's rights, has exceptional presence. She speaks with passion and clarity when she discusses her goal of bringing education to girls around the world. She is absolutely captivating.[3] All these women are fully present, not only in body, but in mind and spirit. Their entire being is engaged in what they are saying.

Presence is not to be confused with charisma. Charisma involves a bit of flash. It is an aspect of certain personalities. Presence comes from a deeper, more personal place. You are not born with it: it's something that can be learned and encouraged. Presence isn't just on the surface; it is an embodiment of what we are, and it's a willingness to share who we are with others—and with our audiences.

Presence involves turning up the dial on our inner energy. This is not nervous energy or excitement, aggression or loudness. A person can have lots of energy and absolutely no presence. You've probably seen speakers who seem to leak energy all over the place. They have a busy, flyaway vigor that's marked by a manic pace but lacks focus. Some women convey this frenetic energy when they are nervous or feel rushed—and in doing so, they project the farthest thing from presence.

Presence involves focusing positive energy that we find within ourselves. The physical center of our energy is in the belly region of our body—our gut, where we feel our nerves, passion, beliefs. We draw our deepest breaths from that area. No one ever expressed conviction in an idea without feeling it deep down. When we connect to our core in a relaxed yet focused way and then offer our messages to our audience, we literally *breathe life* into our ideas. Belief in our ideas creates the energy to deliver them. Think of a time when you felt full of this conviction, when you felt mind and body come together in an undeniable way. This is the kind of focused energy we are striving for when we speak.

Indeed, everything this book has discussed so far is necessary to achieving presence. You can't have physical presence unless you choose to take the stage, create a strong script, and find the voice to fully express those thoughts. Embracing a "taking the stage" mindset and being committed to what you are saying will allow you to turn up the dial within yourself. You will be completely connected to what you are saying in a way that focuses you. In this way, then, presence is not simply a physical state. It is the *physical manifestation* of what is inside you. But it takes the skills discussed in part 4 of this book to *bring all of that inner feeling to the audience*.

Having presence demands that we are "in the moment." Actors use this term to describe what it means to be truly connected to what you are saying, and fully present to your audience. This means not thinking of the past or the future, but being completely engaged in the act of communicating. It means talking to your listeners from the depth of your being. If you do so, you will be present in your voice and in your body; and you will inspire your audience. I am in that "zone" when I go into each client meeting with an absolute focus on winning the business—not just because it's nice to make a sale, but because I'm convinced that it's the best thing for my client. My mind, energy, words, and physical being all work together to bring that message forward—and for me these are exhilarating moments. I feel so alive.

There is nothing worse than listening to someone giving a presentation or conducting a one-on-one meeting and feeling they're not really there. You don't know where they are, they just aren't in the room with you! We sap our energy when we allow our minds to race ahead to waiting emails and endless "to-do" lists. Or if we're giving a presentation and are worried about a mistake made that morning or whether the babysitter will turn up on time, we cannot have presence. Only part of us is engaged. The physical manifestation of this distractedness is a scattered and disjointed speaking style and perhaps a furtive glance at our email. Presence involves *absolute* concentration on the act of speaking. By being present we lead by example. We encourage our listeners to be fully present.

When we offer our audiences our authentic energy, we convey an onstage presence that is unique to each of us. I have coached many successful women over the years and each one has found her own authentic presence. One female executive of an automotive manufacturing firm was physically small and unimposing in her dress and demeanor, but she was grounded in herself and driven by strong convictions. When she got up to speak she made everyone in the room feel privileged to be there. Another female head of a telecommunications firm had a much more flamboyant style. She wore brilliant colors like peacock blue and conveyed natural warmth that was strong and immediate. She drew people to her because of her expansive energy. A third female executive, a banker, was beautifully elegant; she exuded graciousness and poise. What set her apart even more than her polish was her emotional honesty and captivating wit. Listeners always felt she was letting them in on some profound truths about life.

All three women had a strong presence, but in different ways. And that's exactly what you want to find: your own "brand" of presence. You may have a quiet style, but be able to make the entire room feel privileged to be in your presence. Or you may have an outgoing energy that makes others bond with you. Or it may be your grace, elegance, and sense of humor that draws people in. Your presence must be true to who you are and what you believe about yourself.

To convey presence, you can't let anything stand between you and your audience. That includes PowerPoint slides or any other paraphernalia like flip charts. You will not be fully present if you speak with slides; they often dominate the room, and the speaker becomes a mere narrator.

If you have a text with too much detail, the audience only hears "this fact" and "that fact." Your warmth and energy are consumed by the task of trying to communicate that excessive detail. Even a pen in your hand is a distraction. Keep it simple when you speak, so you can come through to your audience.

Finally, a speaker with presence *trusts listeners to respond*—but doesn't view them as judgmental. Women often care—even worry—too much about what the audience thinks of them. It goes back to their common desire to be liked. You must open up to the audience, but not confer on them the power to judge you, like or dislike you, or define you.

Simone de Beauvoir's categories of "Self" and "Other" apply here.[4] In *The Second Sex* she says that women traditionally have been seen as the Other in relation to the Self. But it is not a status we should embrace. Our value is not derivative. When women are speaking, they should see themselves as the focus, the Self, the source of power. When you're on stage, this means seeing yourself confidently as having something important to say—and your audience as being there to respond positively to you. This relationship to your audience will enable you to have presence without feeling vulnerable. It will make you feel that you can be your true authentic self without risking that the audience will judge you. "Self" and "Other" describe a dynamic that can work in your favor if you see yourself as the Self—the one who is center stage.

In sum, presence involves a deep conviction about the importance of your message and an ability to share who you are. Once you have that outlook, the skills discussed in the ensuing chapters will further strengthen your presence and your ability to lead.

Advice for Leaders of Women

This chapter explains the meaning of presence, a defining quality for leaders. You can help women on your team gain a strong presence in the following ways:

- Begin by understanding exactly what *presence* is.
- Become a role model by demonstrating this quality yourself.

- Recognize that "male" and "female" presence may take different forms. But ask yourself, "Do the women on my team have the kind of presence that serves them as leaders?
- If you feel someone lacks that presence, raise this issue one-on-one with her.
- Provide coaching or a seminar for her development.

Chapter Twenty-Two

Be Fearless on Stage

I once observed the president of a remarkable startup grow visibly nervous when a crowd of about two hundred shareholders took their seats for her firm's annual general meeting. As she spoke, she stumbled over her words and apologized. She announced a new contract, and then backtracked and said, "Sorry, I mean a new *partnership*." She noted the company had expanded to 2,400 employees . . . and then corrected herself: "I mean 2,400 employees *worldwide*." What might have been a wonderful speech with much good news about her company became an angst-ridden address.

The challenge she faced—stage fright—is a common one and appears to be more frequent in women than in men. The majority of women I work with tell me they have anxieties about stage fright. But in all my years of teaching and coaching, I've encountered only a smattering of men who told me that they had stage fright. Indeed, when on stage most men seem to have what Columbia Business School terms "honest over-confidence," meaning *they are genuinely convinced they are that good!*[1] Women on the other hand can think of a million reasons not to speak up. And when they are asked to make a presentation or give a speech—they may say "yes" for all the right reasons, but when the time comes they are often in agony—plagued by The Imposter Syndrome and other crippling female diseases.

If you want to speak with power and achieve the presence discussed in the previous chapter, you must dispel these anxieties and strive to be fearless on stage.

Why Do We Fear the Stage?

For many women stage fright is based on a fear that their audience will judge them harshly or see them as inferior in some way. Many even worry that speaking out will make them seem *too powerful*—and that boldness will encourage men and other women to criticize them. Often women appear more comfortable remaining silent in the wings than holding forth on center stage. After all, if we have been taught as girls to "be still" and not raise our voices or sound too strong, there's often a voice inside us saying, "Keep quiet," or "If you speak up, you'll sound foolish or wrong or too full of yourself." In some cases, bosses, husbands, and siblings have reinforced that negative self-concept. But more commonly we do it to ourselves—and then wonder why.

Women are also more inclined than men to have body image issues that keep them from speaking comfortably in the spotlight. As discussed in prior chapters, the women we videotape in our sessions often make observations about their hair or their weight when we play back the tape. Even as the instructor is providing feedback on their speaking and general presence, some women are focused instead on how they can lose ten pounds. They worry that their clothes, their makeup, or even their nails are not right—and they judge themselves harshly because of it.

Although I established a successful company that teaches executives how to speak, and I often address large audiences, I'm no stranger to stage fright. It's a challenge I've worked hard to overcome. I well remember my first experience with those anxieties. I was in seventh grade, and we were learning how to do impromptu speaking. It was trial by fire: no instruction, no guidelines. The teacher simply called upon us (or me—I don't remember anyone or anything else!) and said, "Judy, your topic is BOYS." Being shy made it difficult for me to talk about *anything*—and I definitely did not want to share my inner thoughts about boys, or do so before an audience that had some of them in it! All I remember was blushing and stumbling through my first line, which was "I can't understand why you would ask me to talk about this subject, since I come from a family of five girls!" I would say that under the circumstances, that was a great opening. But I'm not sure that many coherent words followed my grabber.

Nor did these concerns quickly disappear. I had to line up my butterflies when I was a university lecturer addressing large classes. When I started my business, I needed to overcome my stage fright every time I made a cold call to a top executive. I was glad they couldn't see me huddled over the phone, because my crouched body language reflected my anxiety. Even when I address a large group today, I do my best to check my fears in the foyer before I walk into the auditorium. As I explained in the book's introduction, my concerns are heightened because I believe audiences expect that I—the founder and until recently the head of a global communications firm—will be THE BEST. That kind of pressure doesn't go away!

I tell you these stories about myself because they say a lot about the fears many people carry around and also because they show that whatever your background or past experiences, you can become—with determination—a successful center stage speaker. In fact, I believe it was shyness that led me to seek the stage throughout my career and drove me to surmount a challenge that I have worked very hard to master. Today I actually enjoy the spotlight.

What can you do to become more confident on stage?

Becoming Fearless on Stage

There's no magic pill you can take to wish away stage fright. Sometimes just plunging in and speaking with courage is the answer. One woman told me the strength she found when her best friend and brother got married. She explained, "I decided to say something at the wedding. I was certainly nervous—but I made myself do it (after a glass of wine). I used what I had learned in Taking the Stage about slowing down and projecting my voice—and it went well. Everyone said, 'Wow, you're really strong.'"

If you know in advance that you will be speaking, the best solution involves a step-by-step process that includes preparing well before your talk, adopting a positive mindset on the day of the speech, being "in the moment" when speaking, and finally reflecting on how you performed. Let's look at each step in more detail.

Before You Speak: Prepare Well

- *Understand the audience.* As soon as you find out you're going to be speaking, think about what the audience needs to hear from you. Do you want to change their minds? Do you want to instill excitement about some possibility? Do you want to heighten their ability to succeed in some way? In short, how do you want to influence them? Knowing this will give you a *motive* for speaking. And it will take the focus off you, and put it on them!

- *Prepare your best script.* There's a great feeling of comfort in having a powerful text that captures your voice and convictions. Spend time preparing it, walk away and come back to it, and be sure to prepare it *yourself or make it your own if someone else has drafted it.* And prepare even for informal talks, briefings, or client pitches.

- *Rehearse as much as you can.* I'm fortunate to have The Humphrey Group's excellent coaches to work with me on all my major addresses. But even if you don't have such professional help in your firm, you can hire a coach or get valuable feedback by delivering your remarks to a family member, colleague, or friend. Get their views on everything from flow and expression, to eye contact, articulation, and pace.

- *Study TED talks,* especially those given by women. You'll gain new ideas from them. And you'll see that even these brave and capable speakers have a touch of nervousness, which makes them all the more "real."[2]

- *Check out the room* where you will be speaking. Study it. Imagine the audience. Deliver your remarks to that imaginary crowd. And practice in the room if you can.

- *Draw strength from other areas of confidence.* Our instructor, Nicky Guadagni, helped a client achieve a new level of comfort with presenting when she found out that this woman was a state champion horsewoman. Nicky asked her to imagine she was sitting atop her horse. The woman then placed her feet into imaginary stirrups, engaged her legs and pelvis, squared off her shoulders, raised her chest, and commandingly took up the reins by bringing out her hands. According to Nicky, "The transformation was jaw-dropping."

Follow this example and bring the comfort and skills you have in another area—riding a horse, starring in your high school debating society, or chairing a school association—into the boardroom. Visualize yourself with that same strong and commanding presence.

On the Day You Speak: Adopt a Positive Mindset

- If you practice yoga, *try stretches and power poses* that help you feel grounded and expanded.
- Similarly, if you *meditate*, this technique will help you find your strong, still center.[3]
- Know that you look great! Meryl Streep, who once thought, "I was too ugly to be an actress," now advises females not to worry about their weight or appearance. Accept yourself, she urges: "What makes you different or weird, that's your strength . . . I used to worry about my nose, now I don't."[4]
- *Write a mantra* that you can keep repeating to center and calm yourself. For example, you might memorize and repeat to yourself something along the lines of the following: "The young women in the room really need to hear my message!" Or "My presentation will make my audience much stronger leaders." Or "This will be a game changer for these financial advisors."
- *Avoid coffee and all caffeinated beverages* unless you are someone who can have coffee after dinner and sleep like a baby all night. If you add the shot of adrenalin you'll get when you take center stage to the caffeine in your system, you may speed through your script and feel like your heart is in your throat. And you'll probably look nervous and may even shake—not a good image for a speaker!
- *Warm up your voice* in the shower so you have confidence that it will be there for you with volume and range and diction.
- *Rehearse*—even if it only involves saying, "Good morning, my name is . . ." with genuine warmth and eye contact and taking your time with the pace.
- *Mingle with the audience* if you can before the speech. It will humanize them and make you feel more comfortable.

- As you're waiting to speak, take in deep breaths and *concentrate on breathing*.

As You Speak: Be "In the Moment"

- *Know your opening by heart*, look at the audience, and take control of the room.
- *Concentrate* on the thought you are delivering and invest yourself fully in it. Remember: presence comes from "being in the present."
- *Breathe freely.* If you feel nervous as you speak, take a moment to stop and become aware of your breath. Take two or three breaths to bring the air down into your belly.
- *Be slow and conversational.* If it feels like you're going *really* slowly, you are probably speaking at the right pace!
- *Look at the audience* and *pause after each sentence.* We do this naturally in conversation, and it will ensure that you stay calm and connected to your audience. It will also help them think about what you've just said.

After You Speak: Congratulate Yourself

- *Take pride* in your accomplishment, and reflect on all the things you did right. Don't worry that you could have done better. Next time, you will!
- *Seize new opportunities to speak.* Every time you put yourself forward, you will become more comfortable and it will feel more natural.

These strategies will bolster your confidence and give you the poise and presence of a superb speaker. And if you want to gain inspiration from someone who has dealt with stage fright, read the article by Susan Cain called "An Introvert Steps Out: How the Author of 'Quiet' Delivered a Rousing Speech."[5] Susan was one brave woman—a self-professed introvert who gave a TED talk—one of the most high-profile televised speeches a noncelebrity can give. She underwent a year of preparation that consisted of "three stages of accelerated dread." But it culminated in a deeply moving and entertaining speech that you can view on TED Talks.[6]

You may not feel you can spend a year preparing, or that you'll ever be good enough to deliver a TED talk—but if you take the steps discussed in this chapter, you *will* surprise yourself with the confidence you gain. Don't worry if you have not been able to rid yourself of nerves completely; a little nervousness will add to your energy level and give your talk a touch of intensity. And if your audience sees a little nervousness, they will appreciate all the more the courage you are showing!

Courage is the hallmark of the performer. As the playwright, David Mamet, writes, "The actor before the curtain, the soldier going into combat, the fighter into the arena, the athlete before the event, may have feelings of self-doubt, fear, or panic. . . . The rational individual will, when the bell rings, go out there anyway to do the job she said she was going to do. This is called courage."[7]

Advice for Leaders of Women

Stage fright is common to both women and men, but it grips many women more intensely for the reasons discussed in this chapter. They may fear performing on a large stage and even get stage fright when speaking up at a management meeting. Here's what you can do to help:

- If you have any "nerves" of your own, you might share that fact. This will make them feel they are not in this alone.
- If you're chairing a meeting, call on those individuals who have yet to speak. As CEO John Montalbano explains, "In doing so, you invite people to take a personal risk by putting their ideas 'out there.' Generally, what you will observe from individuals who once said little but have now been encouraged to speak is that they begin to naturally contribute in future meetings. Indeed, the chair plays a critical role in bringing out voices that otherwise would stay passive."
- Think about other ways you can encourage a team member to overcome any fears she may have. You might ask her to be the emcee for a

team event or urge her to speak at an industry conference. You can be part of the solution by encouraging these acts of courage.

- Allow her to rehearse before "opening night." Taking the stage, even for actors, requires a lot of practice and rehearsing. Allow your team members to practice with you and give them feedback on their performance.

Chapter Twenty-Three

Sit Tall, Stand Tall

M ei is a tiny woman dressed all in black who sits stock-still when she speaks. Her voice has authority, but physically she seems to disappear. She has been passed over for several promotions, and it's easy to see one reason why: her stance suggests she wants to hide in plain sight. But that's about to change. Our instructor inquires whether she ever played sports. "Well, I was a classically trained ballet dancer for fourteen years," Mei says. Our instructor asks for a short demonstration. Mei removes her black jacket and then stands and performs a perfect ballet move—she takes up the space in an elegant regal way and looks at those in the room with warmth. All are taken by her presence and can't take their eyes off her.

At that moment, something clicks for Mei. She realizes that even though she's petite, she can have a commanding presence. Her strong body language carries over into the presentation she makes that afternoon. Her progress inspires not only Mei but others in the seminar. The point made by her newfound strength is clear: to take the corporate stage, you must sit tall and stand tall.

The Incredible Shrinking Woman

Consider the fact that *status* and *stature* are closely related words. Indeed, research has shown that senior executives tend to be taller than their more junior counterparts—something that's true for both men and women.[1]

When someone stands tall, we view them as having more confidence and conviction, which translates into seeing them as having more stature and deserving respect. We also feel better about ourselves when *we* stand tall.

Despite this correlation between physical stature and respect, women often make themselves small. Although physically less imposing than their male counterparts, women *further shrink themselves*. In our twenty-five years working with women, The Humphrey Group has observed that women frequently minimize themselves physically by taking up only a portion of their chair, sitting with their backs rounded, crossing their legs and ankles, and folding their arms or hands, often hiding them in their laps. This "self-wrap" not only physically diminishes our presence, it also can convey the impression of insecurity or defensiveness.

Anyone with such a weak presence experiences many disadvantages. Others are less likely to look to them for leadership or take their comments as seriously. Furthermore, these in-drawn stances make speaking more difficult. When you hunch forward you squash your ribs, a position that makes it harder to breathe. Your voice has less fuel and others are less likely to hear your ideas. Try this exercise: assume an open position and then squeeze in your shoulders slightly. You'll find it's hard to speak with conviction or to project the confidence of a leader.

Men, by contrast, make themselves larger. When our instructors ask a roomful of women to "sit like men," they immediately expand their chests, stretch out and extend their arms, and rest them on adjacent chairs. They place their feet wide apart and solidly on the ground; they toss their heads back and peruse the room with a sense of ownership. Women easily understand this more powerful body language, but they shrink back into their more compressed forms as soon as the exercise is over. They feel more comfortable assuming a self-protective stance. Sitting or standing like men is not the answer for women. We need to define our own strong stance.

Sit Tall

When sitting, you can develop a more open, confident stance by adopting these guidelines:

- *Take your seat at the table.* If you can control where you sit at a meeting—and very often you can—stay away from the *outer circle and lone chairs and sit at the table*. If you are leading the meeting, sit at the end of the table, preferably facing the door so you can see who is coming in. If you want to create a more inclusive feeling, sit either near the middle of the table or at the end of one side. If you are a participant, position yourself close to the end so you will have a full view of everyone, and they will be able to see you. Boardroom tables are often curved, and the person near the end can see everyone's face without having to turn from side to side.

- *Stay grounded*. You gain power when you *have both feet on the floor*. This means your chair must be exactly the right size for you to plant your feet on the floor. It often doesn't occur to a woman that feeling inconsequential may have something to do with the height of her chair. Holly, a woman of average height, appeared to lack authority during her seated presentation. When she finished it became clear that her feet were not even touching the floor. She readjusted the chair so it was six inches lower and her feet planted themselves on the floor, and she presented again. This time her whole demeanor changed—her voice was deeper, her pace slower, and she spoke with more conviction. She had more gravitas! Women have made do with nonadjustable chairs for decades. But now offices provide adjustable seats. Take the time to make the chair fit you. Even Goldilocks in "The Three Bears" took time to find a chair that was "not too large, not too small, but just right!"

- *Uncross your legs*. Our mothers told us to cross our legs, but doing so casts you in a more passive "listening" position. You'll naturally uncross your legs when you make a point, but do it even before that—as soon as you sit down. Hold your knees close together if you are wearing a skirt. In pants, you can release your knees more, about hip-width apart.

- *Sit tall*. Move back into the chair and feel your sit bones at the bottom of your spine pressed into the seat of the chair. Once you're sitting against the back of your chair, you will naturally "grow" tall—and your posture will be strong. Avoid bending forward from your waist. This is one instance where "leaning in" doesn't work!

How important to your image is sitting tall? Extremely. One woman told us an unusual story about her success in meetings and overall corporate life. She told us that she never slouched at meetings and always sat with grace and elegance, tall in her chair. Her body language announced, "I am present, I am listening, and I am a leader." She retained that position even while others slumped during soporific meetings. When someone asked her how she sustained her powerful stance, she explained, "Oh, that's easy. I've had an operation and I have a metal rod in my back." It worked, but we hope that none of our readers will have to go such lengths to achieve the stance of a leader!

- *Take up the full chair.* Men often take up more than one chair by extending their arms across the chairs next to them. Such outreach is not always appropriate because it encroaches on another person's space. But women need to expand their space and take up *one full chair*. Do this by avoiding the temptation to move to one side of the chair and perch in the corner of the seat. Distribute your weight equally across the chair. You'll never own the room if you don't own the chair!

- *Arm yourself!* How we hold our forearms contributes to our presence. Either put them on *the arms of your chair or extend them onto the table*. Holding these limbs out front gives us more physical presence than keeping them in our laps. So reach out and keep your arms in the "ready" position for gestures. Be sure not to cross your arms or fold your hands, since those positions destroy the open, confident presence you project with arms extended.

- *Be still.* Stillness exudes confidence. We tend to move around too much and fidget when we are nervous or insecure: our heads bob and our bodies sway. Stillness shows confidence and power. It shows we are listening when others are speaking.

- *Eliminate the clutter.* If you want to give yourself presence, take away the array of distracting items in front of you—water bottles, purses, binders, papers, and glasses cases. All you need are your notes if you're speaking and a clean pad for note taking. Look the part of someone who's not just a "worker bee."

In short, look strong when you sit in a meeting. One senior woman summed up much of this advice: "I like to sit tall in my chair with my arms extended onto the table, squaring off in a way that causes people to think, 'She's forceful.' That position conveys more of a sense of urgency than being slumped in your chair. It really makes a statement. Some men might be able to get away with sitting back, relaxed, hooking one arm over the back of their chair—but unless they're the CEO, I don't take them as seriously when they are not sitting up."

A strong stance will enable you to stand out at the table. As one participant said after taking our course, "I noticed that the women who attended are carrying themselves differently in meetings and at the table. It is quite noticeable and impressive." Saravani, an HR manager from Malaysia, echoed this sentiment: "I used to sit in meetings leaning in the chair with both hands on my lap. After attending Taking the Stage, I realized that there is a better body language. We should sit with good posture and place our arms on the handle of the chair or on the table. It reflects higher confidence to the audience. My male colleagues mostly sit in such a manner. Others are now taking me more seriously especially when I am presenting ideas."

Stand Tall

Sitting tall is crucial—but when you can, *stand*. Not only will you *look* more commanding; you will *feel* more in control. You will also have a stronger, clearer voice when you're standing up. So unless you're presenting to a small and informal group, get up on your feet. Even on conference calls, stand up if you are speaking. Your voice will project more energy and confidence. Others might not see you, but they will hear the difference. Stand up wherever possible, and keep the following guidelines in mind when doing so.

- *Plant your feet.* Stand firmly with your feet shoulder-width apart. Feel your legs relaxed yet strong under you. Your knees should be unlocked and bent slightly. Many women have to learn this stance. In one of our seminars, a twenty-something guidance counselor named Brenda gave her presentation with her legs oddly wrapped around each other. It was an extraordinarily unstable pose, and ironic because she was role-playing a speech telling her audience how to help children stand on their own two feet! People expect you as a leader to stand squarely on your own two feet.

- *Stand tall.* I remember walking around my living room as a teenager balancing a book on my head while my mother coached me and my sisters on good posture. We must have made quite a sight! But it was a great exercise. Standing tall is about claiming your stature—whether you are physically short or tall. Think of height as an attitude, not a physical attribute. To achieve this, hold your head high, balance it on a relaxed neck, and drop your shoulders back.

- *Keep your arms relaxed at your sides.* Gestures will come to you more naturally when your arms are at your side because they are "available" to gesture. Never fold or cross your arms. Folding them creates the impression that you're not comfortable with what you're saying or that you are hiding something—or even standoffish. You can't deliver a strong leadership message with crossed arms.

- *Move deliberately.* When you stand, move deliberately to show grace and strength in the steps you take. How much you move depends on the situation. If you're delivering a formal speech behind a podium you may come out from behind the podium, particularly if you're giving a motivational talk. That will suggest openness on your part. But if you are speaking at a bank board meeting, tradition may require you to stand behind the podium the entire time. You should move when you are on an open stage in front of a group; if you remain stone still, you will imply a lack of emotion and commitment to your message. But don't walk around randomly and don't pace. This can be distracting to the audience. Instead, take a step or change your position every once in a while, coordinating that movement with a new idea, a new slide, or a new section of your talk.

Having a strong stance can make all the difference in your career. A woman we coached, Janet, was upset because her career had stalled. It wasn't hard to tell why. Since high school she had felt she was "too tall," so she developed the habit of jutting out her hip to make herself look shorter. Unfortunately this made her come across as too casual when she stood to present and caused her to continually shift her weight from side to side. Her boss never told her, "Janet, I am not going to give you a promotion until you stop jutting your hip out." It doesn't work that way. Her boss will just write in Janet's performance review, "not enough executive presence," and that will be it. For her to win that promotion, she has to embrace her height and claim her stature.

How can you create your own strong stance? Follow the preceding guidelines. They provide a framework that will give you a posture that is upright, relaxed, and open. Observe women who do hold themselves high. If you want to see what "standing tall" looks like, see Melinda French Gates in her TED talk, "What Non-Profits Can Learn from Coca Cola."[2] She projects true stature. And practice the following exercises—they will help you sit tall and stand tall.

Exercise 1: Build Up Your Physical Strength

You can achieve this goal that's so important for the posture of a leader in various ways. Yoga exercises that stretch and strengthen you are valuable. Weight training can also make you stronger, as can jogging, running, or hiking. Or put on your favorite tunes and dance—even just five minutes a day makes a difference.

Exercise 2: Teach Your Body How to Develop Stature When Sitting

Sit far back on a chair and round your back until you're slumped over. Next clasp your hands on your lap and tuck your feet under your chair. Note the impact of that pose. See how it can make you feel deferential and less confident.

Now *build your strong stance* by doing the following:

1. Sit at a table and make sure your chair is properly adjusted so your feet are planted firmly on the floor.
2. Drill your sit bones down through the seat of the chair. (Sit bones are the bones you sit on at the base of your bottom.)
3. Direct your pelvis downward and feel how your spine stretches upward.

(continued)

(*continued*)

4. Notice how your lungs now have space to expand, and how much more confident you feel.

5. Place your hands on the table so they're available to gesture.

Exercise 3: Teach Your Body How to Achieve a Strong Standing Position

Practice giving a presentation in front of a mirror or videotape yourself. Women in our seminars find this feedback useful. That's particularly true when they know what they should be doing—as you now do. So film yourself—with your digital camera or smartphone— and assess your movements, your posture, and your presence as you practice your presentation.

Advice for Leaders of Women

Leaders express their confidence by sitting up and standing tall. The following steps will enable you to help the women on your team develop a strong stance.

- Be a role model. Take notice of how you stand and sit, and use the tips and techniques in this chapter for yourself. You cannot be a credible coach if you are not able to model what "right" looks like.
- Observe how your female employees sit and stand. Some may have excellent body language, but others may compress themselves in ways that make them look less like leaders. This can involve folding their hands or arms, taking up a small space in their chair, keeping their heads down, rounding their back, and using small busy gestures.
- Share your observations during one-on-one conversations. While some leaders of women may feel comfortable doing so, this can be a delicate topic, and if guidance is needed you may want to recommend a coach.
- When you introduce this topic, emphasize the positive—say "you'll be doing more client presentations, so you'll want to be your best."

Chapter Twenty-Four

Strengthen Your Body Language

P eggy bobs her head continually as she speaks—a gesture that would work well to comfort a young child if she were a kindergarten teacher. But Peggy is a corporate banker, and this tendency to nod her head weakens her presence. To still her head, our instructor asks her to stand with her back to a wall and have her head lightly touch the wall as she speaks. Everyone in the workshop is amazed at how much stronger Peggy appears when her head is still. Even though she has to keep reminding herself not to jut her head forward and back, she has learned an important lesson: getting your body movements right, or when necessary maintaining a certain stillness, allows you to take the stage and project confidence and power. Indeed, movements of your head, eyes, mouth, arms, and hands shape the messages you send about yourself.

Head

Watch your head movements—because other people will, and those gestures are a clear indication of your power as a speaker. Women far more than men display ingratiating head gestures rather than holding their heads high.[1] As the example above suggests, many women nod when speaking. They also nod when listening. This behavior is evident not only among women in the corporate world, but even in nightly newscasts. Watch closely and you'll see how many times female reporters nod their head in agreement even when there is no reason to do so. Our fondness for reinforcing others is usually what prompts us to do this. It falsely suggests we agree—even when we don't. And it results in our coming across as nice and agreeable, rather than authoritative and leader-like. So NO NODDING!

Still another head gesture that weakens our presence is cocking our heads. Why do we do this? Our intention is often to show empathy or to soften our appearance. What this movement actually does is weaken the speaker and lower her status in the relationship. It reminds me of what happens when we ask our dogs if they want to go for a walk and they listen with that adorable ears-up head tilt. They're giving the owner all the power and waiting to see what their master will decide. In the same way, cocking your head suggests submissiveness or deference.

You can avoid these weak head gestures and project a commanding presence by assuming an aligned stance, with shoulders held slightly back and the head upright. Don't bob, nod, or cock your head. Examples of women who display a strong presence and keep their heads high and still include CNN newscaster Christiane Amanpour, First Lady Michelle Obama, and Angela Merkel, chancellor of the Federal Republic of Germany. View them on YouTube; all three demonstrate confident leadership.

Eyes

Strong eye contact is crucial for leaders everywhere. We demonstrate confidence, strength, and respect when we look a person directly in the eyes and show that we value that individual. That visual link is an imperative for leaders around the world, not just in the West. The Humphrey Group teaches women in Europe, the Middle East, and Asia, as well as in the Americas. Women everywhere want to develop strong eye contact as part of their leadership capabilities.

Research sheds light on how we use our eyes. It shows that high-status people tend to look longer at people they're talking to than lower-status individuals do.[2] Studies also indicate that we do not look people in the eye as much as we should. Adults typically make eye contact 30–60 percent of the time in an average conversation, whereas they should be making eye contact 60–70 percent of the time.[3]

Often women—when they do make eye contact—use their eyes in ways that undercut their leadership. We see some raise their eyebrows and bat their eye lashes when they speak. These coquettish gestures may well appeal to the audience in a traditionally feminine way—positioning the female speakers as objects rather than subjects. These women appear to be asking for approval rather than feeling sufficient within themselves. One client batted her eyes, raised her eyebrows regularly, cocked her head, and prettied up her voice—she told me it was because she was worried about being too aggressive. She felt the audience would like her "softer" style. Although some individuals in the audience might welcome this behavior, their approval comes at the expense of respect for the speaker's leadership and authority.

Some women also weaken their style by using furtive or fleeting eye contact. When we do not look others squarely in the eyes and hold their gaze, they tend to regard us as lacking in confidence. We also observe women who open their eyes wide to emphasize a point—the visual equivalent of saying "Wow!" or "Gee whiz!"—not a very effective gesture for a leader.

You want strong, sustained, warm, and animated eye contact. Looking directly into the eyes of the person you are talking to longer than you normally would is a way of saying, "I am sure of myself; I know what I'm saying; and I want you to hear it." I remember an interaction that took place early in my business career: I was standing in front of an elevator and when the doors opened, the chief executive officer of the company stepped out. While I of course knew him by reputation, he didn't know me. Yet he fixed his eyes on mine with such intensity that I remember his gaze to this day. I believe he really wanted to know me. Strong eye contact sends a clear message to others about the relationship you want with them. It tells them you are confident in what you can bring.

I've always noticed that when I meet with new executive clients, they look at me firmly, testing me to see how long I return their gaze. This is an expression of their power and a test of mine. This kind of steady eye contact need not be severe or intimidating. Think of it as a "greeting" that builds rapport—and is particularly important at the executive level.

Mouth

Smiling and the warmth it conveys are an important part of communication not just among close friends, but also in the business world. Still, you want to get this one right—because there *can* be too much of a good thing.

Some women smile too much. We often observe them delivering business presentations with the corners of their mouth turned upward. They may say (smiling), "We need to cut costs and reduce expenditures if we are to reach our profitability targets." What message will the audience take away? Their happy faces override their words, and people will assume that their leader is sweet but not serious.

That constant smile derives from females' socialization. Sometimes others ask us to smile in an attempt to turn us into good little girls or attractive feminine beings rather than colleagues or leaders. One of our instructors cohosted a TV show and the director asked her to smile, but never asked the male cohost to do so. And who among us has not had someone come up to us when we're thinking through a serious issue and tell us to smile? It's maddening. We don't want to lose our animation; but we don't want to bow to those who see women simply as happy faces!

Smiling, particularly when it's continuous or inappropriate, undercuts leadership. Research by Timothy Ketelaar, associate professor of psychology at New Mexico State University, indicates that "across the few animal species that smile, [the smiles] seem to be advertising that the displayer is not a threat to more dominant individuals. In the case of social prestige, smiles seem to be providing a similar function, provoking strategic deference." For that reason, "higher status individuals lose some of [their] power by smiling."[4]

The answer certainly isn't to go through life stone-faced. In fact, some of the women we coach need *more* animation and facial warmth, because an animated face can lead to a more expressive voice (and we already know how crucial that is!). That is why it's important to warm up your facial expression even when you are speaking on a conference call. But your smiles should be strongly connected to the substance you present. There's no reason to have a happy face if your remarks focus on a tough but necessary corporate restructuring. But if you're thanking your team for splendid results, let your feelings shine. When you do show that warmth, think of speaking with an "inner smile" and let that be your true source of animation. Your smile should be part of your excitement, conviction, and leadership. It will reflect the vibrancy that is evident throughout your whole body.

Arms and Hands

We in The Humphrey Group are often asked, "What should I do with my arms and hands?" While our arms and hands somehow seem to know what to do when we are walking around and talking to friends, we view them as awkward appendages the second we get in front of an audience. We may feel uncomfortable and fold them in front of us when we are standing or sitting or clamp them to our sides at the elbows, creating a flipper movement as we gesture. Or we might grab the podium and hold on for dear life. Such stances create "closed" body language that makes us appear defensive, awkward, and insecure.

Dan Dumsha, a senior instructor in The Humphrey Group who conveys extraordinary presence, explains what to do with your arms and hands:

> If you're standing when you present, begin by "taking your space." Plant your feet about shoulder-width apart, relax your arms and hands at your sides—not in fists, pointing or holding anything. Lift your head, make eye contact, smile, take that deep breath, and say, "Good morning." This will anchor you.
>
> Once you begin speaking, bring your arms up and let your hands be free for open and sustained gestures that complement your words. The resting place for your hands is now above your waist, with the palms facing towards the audience. This is reminiscent of the greeting ritual in many First Nations bands who welcome others with open hands to signify bearing no weapons. We also call this the "beach ball" technique—as if you are gently tossing a big beach ball to the audience when you propose an idea or message. Your hands can go back to the strong anchor position at your sides when you are not gesturing; you can then lift, extend, and sustain them as appropriate.

By combining the two techniques of hands at the sides and above the waist in sustained open-offering gestures, a speaker conveys natural and authentic leadership. These movements indicate that you're open, present, and energized.

Use the same principles when sitting at a meeting. Begin with your hands resting gently on the arm rests or table. Then bring them forward when you make a point, much as you might do when standing (imagine holding a slightly smaller beach ball). When you have finished making your point, bring your hands and arms down to the resting position.

Whether standing or sitting, avoid small, busy gestures such as hand wringing or tossing your hands outward from the wrists. Keep your hands still if you are not making a point or if you are simply listening. Don't fix your hair or fiddle with your clothing or jewelry. Such "grooming gestures" suggest that we are seeing ourselves as objects, not subjects. And resist the weak and self-effacing gestures of covering your face, eyes, or mouth with your hand.

But don't worry about being *too* expressive; most people err by not gesturing enough. Women often say to us, "I'm Italian, or South Asian, or Mexican. I use my hands too much"—yet our instructors rarely feel this is the case. There is no one version of gestures that's right for everyone, and you don't want to hide your true self or pretend to be someone else when presenting or speaking. You may freely express yourself as long as your gestures help you make your point and don't distract. Watching yourself on videotape will help you get the balance right. You'll find that you look more impressive and persuasive as you strengthen your gestures.

And *do* use your hands to reach out to others with a handshake. If you are in a networking situation or are meeting a client or someone new, extend your hand, introduce yourself with your first and last name—pronouncing these words loudly and proudly—and look the person directly in the eye and *hold the eye contact*. The handshake has traditionally been an important aspect of business etiquette, and you should use it to your advantage.

Body language—the way we use our head, eyes, mouth, arms, and hands—is a vital part of communicating to others. Get this idiom wrong, and you'll distract listeners and undercut your message. But master this language, and you'll find that you will bring extraordinary power and presence to your speaking.

Advice for Leaders of Women

We use our bodies to express our thoughts. But our body language can hinder self-expression and undermine our leadership image. Women's body language may be strong and confident, but if not, you can help in a number of ways:

- Be a role model yourself. Study the techniques in this chapter.
- Notice behaviors that undercut leadership. These may include head nodding or bobbing; furtive, inappropriate, or distracting eye contact; fake smiles; arms and hands that move too much or too little; and busy gestures.
- You may wish to take the individual aside and delicately provide a coaching moment. Show her what would work better.
- Offer professional coaching.

Chapter Twenty-Five

She's Smart . . . but She Doesn't Look It

I once coached a female vice president, Marcia, who had risen high in a male-dominated industry. I happened to be talking to a senior executive in her company early in our relationship and asked him what he thought of my client. He replied, "She's smart, but she doesn't look it." My jaw dropped!

"What do you mean?" I asked.

"She's . . . girly," he said.

Once I thought about it, I could see what he meant. Marcia was an attractive woman in her late thirties. She had long hair draped over her face and slight cleavage showing from low-cut silk blouses. One could say she was calling attention to her sexuality. And that can be dangerous.

We can learn two lessons from that comment: (1) Women are being watched and judged—though not necessarily with negative intent; (2) Looks are important in business. Any discordant messages you send with your clothing or appearance can undermine the way executives view you and stall your career. This chapter presents six rules for looking like a leader. These will help women deal with the challenge of "dressing for success." A polished appearance is an important step toward achieving presence.

Rule 1. Dress for Your Corporate Environment

When deciding how to dress for work, and in selecting any particular item, know that one size does not fit all. Your proper attire is dramatically different if you're a bank vice president than if you're part of a Silicon Valley startup. A skirted suit and tailored blouse would be as out of place in a small tech firm as jeans and a hoody would be in a major law firm. (Of course, if you're in the top ranks of a tech firm, and spend your days with bankers and lawyers, you'll dress more like those clients.)

So *get to know your environment*. Like the member of any species, you survive best when you fit in. If your company has formal dress codes, follow them. Clifford Chance, one of the largest law firms in the world, released a memo in which women were told not to be too sexy ("If wearing a skirt, make sure people can't see up it") and were also instructed not to be too dull ("Don't dress like a mortician").[1] Similarly, Swiss financial services company UBS issued a forty-four-page document in 2010 on clothing standards for women and men, including the color of underwear women should wear (neutral). UBS's guidelines were mocked as being too rigid, and it was forced to reissue them in a shorter format.[2] Informal codes are more common and often take precedent over written ones, which can have a short shelf life. As an employee, you must be sensitive to those changes, such as the spread of "casual Fridays." But don't be fooled into thinking that traditional garb is no longer required. When one client wore cowboy boots to the office, her boss singled her out as needing "grooming."

National cultures also shape corporate environments. There are differences—sometimes subtle, sometimes striking—in the way business-people in different countries dress. Because The Humphrey Group trains around the world, we regularly observe these variations. Some places have brighter colors and fancier shoes; for instance, we see some amazing footwear on the women directors we teach in Mexico. These women often wear high heels with two or three tones and wild patterns. We asked, "Why the fancy shoes?" "Many of us are short," they replied. "Our shoes make us feel more powerful and more beautiful." Still the same basic principle applies everywhere: observe your environment and dress accordingly.

Rule 2. Dress for the Job You Want

You've likely heard this one before, but one of the best ways to get ahead is to dress for the position *you want*—not the one you have. I meet many female middle managers who aspire to be VPs. But too often they dress down rather than up. They may wear dresses that lack elegance or the power to inspire. (Yes—even our clothing should inspire.) They wear jackets that may not match their dress, skirt, or pants—a makeshift look that says, "I'm too busy to bother pulling together an elegant outfit" or "I work behind the scenes, so I don't have to dress well."

If you want to advance your career, look the part of a confident leader. Cultivate a pulled-together appearance that has overall unity, structure, and relies on quality materials. A suit, a dress and matching sweater or jacket, or a coordinated look is always appropriate in an office where the men wear suits. And don't leave your shoes out of the equation. They should complement your look and be part of your polished appearance. The quality of the fabric and workmanship, too, say a lot about how you see yourself. You should always look your best—at any level. You may not want to look like an executive if you're a plant manager—people would wonder why you are pretending to be one—but you can don a well-pressed pair of pants or a jacket for a meeting.

You might find you're spending more for clothing than before. But consider those outfits an investment. If you dress as though you have a VP's salary, you are more likely to get that job. Your boss and other executives will see you as already looking the part. As you spend more, you'll likely also find more interesting clothing—clothing with flair, perhaps a suit that has elegant lines or a touch of color. People will see that you're developing your own authentic style and the character to assume a leadership role.

Observe the women who set the standard in your industry and company. If you are in Silicon Valley, look at leaders like Marissa Meyer or Sheryl Sandberg—women who stand at or near the top of Yahoo and Facebook. You may feel you can't afford to dress like these C-level executives—but you can copy their look on a more modest budget. You'll get a sense of what works by looking at how these women dress, and by studying other C-level executives and VPs.

Rule 3. Dress for the People You'll See

If you're meeting with clients or executives, or addressing an audience, those individuals become your reference point rather than the people in your office. I learned that lesson when I was a speech writer. I could be called into our CEO's office to discuss a speech on any given day; so I dressed as though I was going to the executive suite every day, typically in a quality suit and heels.

If you're giving a presentation, dress for that audience. Cindy, a logistics manager, told me about giving a presentation that had gone very well.

"What do you think made your presentation such a success?" I asked her.

"Understanding what I was saying, speaking clearly, *and* dressing well that day."

"What did you wear?" I inquired.

"I had on tailored slacks, a nice shirt, and a new pair of shoes; it was very professional."

You don't always know what meetings you'll have on a given day, so leave an upscale outfit in your office. One senior woman named Nadine said, "If I am running a meeting and want to fill an extra seat or two, I'll grab two junior trainees, and tell them to put a jacket on. Some young women wear tights and tunics in the office—which looks great, but I couldn't let them into a meeting with a CEO wearing that. So soon after I hired them, I let them know they should keep a jacket handy at all times." Be prepared. You always want to be properly attired when you meet senior people.

Rule 4. Shun Sexy If You Want to Get Ahead

Don't send mixed messages to your audience by dressing in a provocative manner. In 2010 a thirty-three-year-old Citibank employee, Debralee Lorenzana, was fired despite her excellent track record—because her appearance was too distracting to her male colleagues. HR asked her to stop wearing form-fitting turtlenecks and tight skirts.[3] When she refused to accede to the bank's demands, she was let go, and the arbitrator upheld the decision.[4]

The fact is that we're all judged by the way we dress. Anyone wearing sexy clothing is telling those they meet to pay attention to their physical attributes rather than valuing their abilities as a leader. One bank HR director explained to me how women who dress this way lose their status as professionals: "There are distinct groups of women in our organization: administrative assistants, managers, traders, analysts, and sales people. All these women can get lumped together in people's minds. But the successful ones distinguish themselves by dressing in smart, tailored outfits rather than pencil skirts and provocative blouses."

And the same protocol applies to men. As one male senior executive told me: "It would not be appropriate if I were to come into the office and have two or three buttons on my shirt undone showing chest hair. Women have to play by the same rules." These unspoken rules are for us to look the part of a leader, and wear clothing that does not send any discordant messages. Being attractive is a great thing! But sexiness does not play well to our leadership goals. Don't feel you have to be drab or dowdy. But do shun "sexy."

Rule 5. Beware Bangs and Bangles

Make certain your hair, jewelry, and accessories do not distract from your leadership presence. How we have our hair cut and shaped (and for some, colored) is of great importance. In fact, when one of our instructors asked a client, "How do you prepare for your speeches?" her reply was, "I get my hair done." Many women do just that—and it's no more an "anything goes" world for hair than it is for clothing. Be sure your hair looks professional—not messy, not too "big," or too long. Your hair should fit with your professional appearance, not create a distraction. You want people to focus on your *ideas* not on your hair!

Long hair ideally should be pulled back. A client was on her way to a luncheon one day, and her long mane of hair, which was normally pulled back, fell loose in flowing curls around her face and neck. She looked more like a twenty-year-old than the forty-year-old she was. I commented to her that her usual style looked more corporate. She replied, "Well, it's just a luncheon for our department." As I walked away from her, I wondered if I was being too prescriptive. But she told me later on she was called unexpectedly after the luncheon to a meeting of senior executives—and the CEO gave her a kiss on the cheek when that gathering broke up.

It seemed likely that he was reading her as younger and more feminine, giving her the sort of attention that would not help her career.

In sum, your hair should be suited to your professional stature. One of my clients, a swimmer, explained, "I keep my long hair straight because I swim before I come to work." But she looked like a flower child from the 1960s, and it's no wonder she was repeatedly passed over for promotion to the VP level because her boss said she "lacked presence." Her hair was sending a message, and it wasn't the one that would get her promoted.

Bangles, or any jewelry that calls attention to itself, also will interfere with your leadership image. You do *not* want to take the stage with dangly earrings or big necklaces. Sparkling jewelry will take attention away from you. Save those accessories for nonbusiness occasions when it's okay to leave people with the thought, "That was a great necklace" or "I really liked those earrings." Those are not the messages you want to send your audience in the boardroom.

Rule 6. Follow the First Five Rules—but Develop Your Own Style

Rule 6 doesn't *quite* say ignore rules 1 through 5. But it does say, internalize them and interpret them with your own personal touch. There's no reason that your clothing should be dull if you dress in an appropriate corporate manner. When I began The Humphrey Group in 1988, my professional clothing of choice was the skirted suit, typically in navy or black. Sometimes I would accessorize it with a string of pearls or a little silk tie. That was the number 1 recommendation in all the dress-for-success books back in the 1980s. Although there are still many suits in my wardrobe, they have a lot more flair than those early outfits, as do the dresses I wear. One of my favorite designers for business dress is Nanette Lepore. You can also achieve a professional look from designers like Hugo Boss, Ann Taylor, and Anne Klein. They create high-quality women's clothing that looks professional but is also interesting. There's no reason that playing by the rules has to be dull. My suits and dresses allow me to be comfortable with myself and with any group I'm talking to.

Indeed, your clothes will evolve over the different stages of your career. You can get away with more daring outfits as you rise through the ranks. While waiting to meet an executive at a major bank, I overheard a wonderful exchange between a senior woman and a younger colleague. The young woman said to her, "I have a client to meet on Friday and I don't know what to wear, can you help me?" The senior woman said, "Wear something black, not too sexy, that isn't short or low-cut." Then she said, "I'm at the point that I wear whatever I want. But if I were younger I would definitely try to fit the mold. When you're young and meeting a client, you don't want to be the one standing out. But you have more flexibility when you get to be senior. You can't wear a bright red suit early in your career. At the stage I'm at in my career, I would wear a bright red suit. But that takes years of experience."

So follow the rules, but know when to modify them. More broadly, these six guidelines will serve you well throughout your career. They will help you strengthen your appearance—which will contribute to your success in taking the stage. They will give you a polished presence that tells your audience that you value yourself. And if you wonder whether clothes, hair, and general appearance make a difference in one's likelihood of getting ahead, just look at your executive team and what they wear. Being daring and courageous is important in business, but not in the area of dress or hairstyle! Save your courage for moments when you want to speak up and be heard.

Advice for Leaders of Women

Dress is an issue for both men and women who need to look the part of a leader. Because women have a wider range of wardrobe choices, dress can be a tough issue for them when it comes to career advancement. Although you may not want to broach the topic of dress, it's important to do so if you believe one of your team members is not projecting an image that reflects well upon her and your organization. There are many things you can do to help women in this area.

- Realize that dress is a business issue—not just a personal choice.
- Observe whether women on your team are making the commitment to dress in a polished, professional way.

- If there are some who are not, you have several options: (1) speak to them yourself; (2) ask HR to speak with them; (3) find an image consultant who can help.
- If you hear comments about how sexy or hot a woman is, shut these down. According to Barbara Annis and John Gray in their book, *Work with Me*, this behavior may not be meant to offend. "Many of the comments made toward women are almost reflexive and meant as praise."[5] But such a representation of women can be offensive in business. It's your responsibility to deal with the situation by (1) talking with the male involved; (2) approaching the female involved; and (3) setting standards of mutual respect for your entire team.

Conclusion

The World Is Your Stage

You have now discovered how to take the stage—and make a difference in your career and life. Taking the stage may begin with simple acts of courage on the corporate stage—like raising your hand, asking for a promotion, and having your voice heard. But your impact will extend to others in the corporation, in your family, and in your community. In changing yourself, you can change the world! I have come across so many heartwarming accounts of women who have taken the stage and made a difference in their own lives and in the lives of others.

I have shared with you the results of The Humphrey Group's work with women around the world. These pages have offered insights on how to speak up, stand out, and succeed as strong, confident leaders. This involves developing a center stage *mindset*; a strong *script*; a powerful *voice*; and a confident *presence*. But knowing these techniques is just the beginning. You have to *live* the learning; put this instruction into practice every day if you truly want to take the stage. And that requires commitments similar to those an actor makes—from understanding your role, to learning your lines, to taking a bow.

Let's look at how you play your part from here on.

Always on Stage

To take the stage—again and again—means performing as a leader whether you're at work, at play, or at home. William Shakespeare was correct when he wrote "all the world's a stage, and all the men and women merely players."[1]

You are on the corporate stage every time you give a presentation, speak at a meeting, or have a corridor conversation. Others are watching, listening, and forming opinions of your leadership. And such performances don't stop when you leave work. Others, too, need our leadership. So use the techniques you have learned in this book every time you speak.

The metaphor of the stage has never been more "real" than it is today.

As Rosabeth Moss Kanter writes about today's innovative leaders, "They must be willing to take on unfamiliar roles, think on their feet, pay attention to several things at once, walk into situations for which they are not prepared, and ad lib. This is no job for amateurs."[2] So even though the scene changes, the set changes, the characters change, and the audience changes . . . you have your part to enact every day. It's a role that will show others you are a strong and confident leader.

Develop Your Character

If you want to flourish on center stage, you'll need to develop your "character." This book has emphasized qualities that will help you succeed, such as confidence, courage, and assertiveness. We've discussed other virtues, such as warmth, energy, presence, and the ability to listen well. Much of the book explains how you can cultivate these strengths.

And as any good actor knows, those qualities must come from within. In the words of playwright David Mamet, "That person on stage is *you*. It is not a construct you are free to amend or mold. It's you. It is *your* character which you take onstage."[3] Developing your character therefore means discovering *within yourself* those leadership qualities we have discussed in this book and finding your own way of expressing them. This is exactly what an actor does in preparing for a role.

The leadership qualities discussed in *Taking the Stage* are not always ones that we're born with, or even ones we might think are currently part of our makeup. But as this book's many stories about women—and my own life—indicate, we can *all* develop courage, confidence, and assertiveness. You can improve your voice and your presence. When you *show* strength, you *become* stronger. So think of every moment as an opportunity to develop your leadership character. If you are offered a promotion, as one of my friends was, and you are about to respond, as she was, "Oh no, I'm not ready for it!"—*stop yourself*. The timid, unsure individual is not the role you want to play. Know you were chosen because you are ready for a bigger part! Play the strong role. Give yourself aspirational goals. With each scene seek out new opportunities to shine.

One woman named Jane did just that. She told me that when her father passed away she said to herself, "I am going to give the speech for our family, and though it's going to be difficult, I *will* do it!" In the past she would have deferred to her brothers, one of whom was a radio talk show host and the other was a sports commentator. But she prepared and practiced, and gave her speech to four hundred people. She received many compliments, and her brothers said, "We didn't know you could do things like that." She told me, "Only I (and the choir behind me) knew that my legs were shaking." Developing your role is difficult and exacting. But moments like that encourage us to look within ourselves and see that we can do it!

Learn Your Lines

Actors don't necessarily memorize their lines word by word. Instead, they read the script looking for its "thought lines." And that's a good way to master your scripts. Whatever the occasion, think of your text in terms of The Leader's Script, and break your script down into the elements of that template.

And prepare well. Actors spend enormous amounts of time learning their lines. They may practice their scripts in the shower or walking around their neighborhoods. For a speech or a presentation, give yourself a few weeks to practice. For brief remarks you may need only an evening (or you may learn your lines on the way to the event). For an elevator conversation or Q&A—your prep time may be only a few seconds.

But don't just learn your lines: think of how you will express them. This book has emphasized the fact that women often wish to sound "nice," "obliging," and "nonthreatening." It won't serve you well to continue delivering your lines in this way. Accept that you need to be stronger and more confident in the way you sound. Your character has a bigger part to play . . . and your lines are stronger.

Know Your Objective

Actors are always governed by an "intention" or objective. Everything they do in a play or on screen is shaped by that objective. That goal gives power to their scripts, invigorates their words, and gives a meaning to their presence. And if you want to succeed on the corporate stage—or any other stage—be sure of what your objective is.

Have a goal for every meeting. Think what impact you want to have. It might be a customer sale, a commitment from an employee, approval for a project. The more focused you are, the more you will succeed.

Have a goal for every relationship. An actor knows exactly what he or she wants from each person on the stage, and that intention carries through to the end of the play and motivates that performer. You are on stage, too, so have a clear objective—both short and long term—for your relationships with everyone around you.

Have a goal, too, for your career. Know your ability; know where you want to go; and then take the steps to achieve that goal. An actor never stops auditioning. Put yourself forward for every opportunity and give each "audition" your all. This is the way to build your career.

Life Is a Performance

Your efforts to take the stage shouldn't end when you leave the office. Take the stage at home too.

A business owner in Mexico City coached her daughter, Ruth, with remarkable success. Ruth was a student who had created a photographic essay about migrant women. She pitched it to several newspapers, but had been repeatedly turned down. One day, Ruth visited her mom in Mexico City, and her mom told Ruth how to use The Leader's Script to promote her project. Ruth said she "promptly scripted my presentation and targeted the most prominent newspaper I could think of—the *New York Times*. The clarity I gained on how to present myself and my project enabled me to land an interview with the *Times*. The essay was approved for publication, and appeared in March 2013."[4]

Think of reaching out, too, to people in your community. Isabelle Nizincourt, a Humphrey Group instructor, brought Taking the Stage to a woman in a Mexican prison. Silvia, a thirty-year-old prison inmate, had been granted a five-minute hearing in front of a judge to plead her case for an early release from her ten-year sentence. Isabelle helped Silvia rewrite her script, transforming it from "a rambling victim's tale" into "the script of a victor." The new version made it clear that Silvia holds herself accountable for what she did and is committed to her rehabilitation. She concludes with a strong call to action. The result was that "instead of being given five minutes to plead her case, she was granted twenty minutes. Silvia is now awaiting the verdict with great hopes her appeal will be granted."

As you take the stage, realize that you have an enormous opportunity to reach out to many people—not only executives, bosses, colleagues, and business partners, but those in your family and community. Help them all see that women can be strong, confident leaders.

Take a Bow

After every performance, take a bow! Being on stage is a demanding, exacting, continuous responsibility. Be proud of yourself. When someone congratulates you for a job well done or thanks you for your leadership, accept that you have made a difference. David Mamet writes that when someone says to a performer, "'You were great tonight,' . . . the correct response is 'Thank you very much.' . . . If they enjoyed it, you, the actor, have done your job."[5] So when people—a boss, an employer, a colleague, a spouse, a friend, or a community group—applaud you for taking the stage— accept the praise. Take a bow. You deserve it!

Life can be a great performance if you think of yourself as being on stage and seeing every speaking situation as an opportunity to inspire your audience. But to make the most of each situation, develop your character, learn your lines well, have a clear objective, reach out to key audiences, and welcome the praise. You will come to see *taking the stage* as a way of life—a real-life drama in which you play a central character. You have an opportunity to inspire the world with your leadership. Let your colleagues, bosses, executives, family, and community see you as a great performer who has a center stage role. Companies need to have us in those lead roles—and our families and communities need our leadership. It's time for us to claim our place on center stage. As we do so, we will discover in ourselves a stronger, clearer, more influential voice that can change us, change others, change our companies, and change the world. What are we waiting for? Let's take the stage.

Notes

Introduction

1. Judith Humphrey, "Taking the Stage: How Women Can Achieve a Leadership Presence," *Vital Speeches of the Day*, May 1, 2001, 435–38.
2. Katty Kay and Claire Shipman, *The Confidence Code: The Science and Art of Self-Assurance—What Women Should Know* (New York: HarperCollins, 2014).
3. Judy B. Rosener, "Ways Women Lead," *Harvard Business Review*, November–December 1990, 3–4.
4. Sarah Dinolfo, "High Potentials in the Pipeline: Leaders Pay It Forward," *Catalyst Research Release*, June 13, 2012.
5. John Gerzema and Michael D'Antonio, *The Athena Doctrine: How Women (and the Men Who Think Like Them) Will Rule the Future* (San Francisco: Jossey-Bass, 2013), 8. In a proprietary global survey, the authors found that 66 percent of adults agree that "the world would be a better place if men thought more like women."
6. Phyllis Korkki, "For Women, Parity Is Still a Subtly Steep Climb," *New York Times*, October 8, 2011. Korkki quotes Ilene H. Lang, president and chief executive officer of Catalyst, who refers to "entrenched sexism" and "social norms that are so gendered and so stereotyped that even though we think we've gone past them, we really haven't."
7. Kelvin Pollard, "The Gender Gap in College Enrollment and Graduation," Population Reference Bureau, www.prb.org/Articles/2011/gender-gap-in-education.aspx.
8. Stephanie Coontz, "The Myth of Male Decline," *New York Times*, September 30, 2012, 5.
9. Pollard, "The Gender Gap in College Enrollment and Graduation," 1.
10. Many sources point to this conclusion. Catalyst tells us that in Fortune 500 companies in 2013 women represented only 4.2 percent of CEOs, compared with 2.4 percent in 2009, and they represented 14.3 percent of executive officers in 2012, compared with 13.5 percent in 2009. See Catalyst, "Women in U.S. Management and Labor Force," Knowledge Center/Catalyst.org, http://catalyst.org

/knowledge/women-us-management-and-labor. Grant Thornton in 2012 stated, "Women hold one in five senior management roles globally, very similar to the level observed in 2004." See *The 2012 Grant Thornton International Business Report*, "Women in Senior Management: Still Not Enough," www.internationalbusinessreport .com/files/ibr2012%20-%20women%20in%20senior%20management%20master .pdf. *The Rosenzweig Report on Women at the Top Levels of Corporate Canada* shows that women in the named officer position of the top 100 biggest public companies in Canada have risen from 4.6 percent to only 8 percent over the past nine years, www .rosenzweigco.com/mediacenter/diversity/index.html. Catherine Rampell states in a *New York Times* article, "Still Few Women in Management, Report Says," September 27, 2010: "As of 2007, the latest year for which comprehensive data on managers was available, women accounted for about 40 percent of managers in the United States work force. In 2000, women held 39 percent of management positions." These data are from a Government Accountability Office report issued in 2012. Barbara Kellerman, a professor of leadership at Harvard's Kennedy School, writes in "The Abiding Tyranny of the Male Leadership Model—a Manifesto," *Harvard Business Review*, April 27, 2010: "I'm sick of hearing how far we've come. I'm sick of hearing how much better situated we are now than before . . . The fact is that so far as leadership is concerned, women in nearly every realm are nearly nowhere." Quoted in Hanna Rosin, *The End of Men*, New York: Riverhead Books, 2012, 198. A biennial survey from Columbia Business School and the Women's Executive Circle of New York, released in November 2013, found that the number of women leading top New York companies had flat-lined in recent years. See Mara Gay, "Women See Slow Progress in Leadership," *Wall Street Journal*, November 14, 2013. See also Philip N. Cohen, "Jump-Starting the Struggle for Equality," *New York Times*, Sunday, November 24, 2013, 9. Cohen writes that "the movement toward equality stopped. The labor force hit 46 percent female in 1994, and it hasn't changed much since. Women's full-time annual earnings were 76 percent of men's in 2001, and 77 percent in 2011." Phyllis Korkki in "For Women, Parity Is Still a Subtly Steep Climb," *New York Times*, October 8, 2011, writes, "Last year, women held about 14 percent of senior executive positions at Fortune 500 companies, according to the non-profit group Catalyst . . . That number has barely budged since 2005, after 10 years of slow but steady increases." Finally, see Nancy M. Carter and Christine Silva's article, "Women in Management: Delusions of Progress," *Harvard Business Review*, March 2010. The authors cite Catalyst research that shows "among graduates of elite MBA programs around the world—the high potentials on whom companies are counting to navigate the turbulent global economy—women continue to lag men at every single career stage, right from their first professional jobs. Reports of progress in advancement, compensation, and career satisfaction are at best overstated, at worst just plain wrong." See full report at www.catalyst.org/publication/ 372/pipelines-broken-promise.

11. Coontz, "The Myth of Male Decline," 5.
12. In a 2011 study, Catalyst found that "companies with the most women board directors outperformed those with the least on return on sales (ROS) by 16 percent and return on invested capital (ROIC), by 26 percent." Cited in "Why Diversity Matters," Catalyst Information Center, www.wgea.gov.au/sites/default/files/Catalyst_Why_diversity_matters.pdf.
13. Warren Buffett, "Warren Buffett Is Bullish . . . on Women," *Fortune*, May 20, 2013, 121, 124.

Chapter One

1. Deborah Tannen, *Talking from 9 to 5: Women and Men at Work* (New York: Quill, 2001), 42.
2. Adam Bryant, "Corner Office: Women and Leadership," *New York Times*, Sunday, October 13, 2013, 6.
3. Patsy Rodenburg, "*Powerspeak*: Women and Their Voices in the Workplace," in *Well-Tuned Women: Growing Strong through Voicework*, ed. Frankie Armstrong and Jenny Pearson (London: Women's Press, 2000), 100–101.

Chapter Two

1. Marion Woodman, *Addiction to Perfection: The Still Unravished Bride* (Toronto: Inner City Books, 1982), 7.
2. Arianna Huffington, *On Becoming Fearless: . . . In Love, Work, and Life* (New York: Little, Brown, 2006), 15.
3. Vanessa Farquharson, "Modesty Is the Best Policy," *National Post*, September 30, 2008, AL 2.
4. Peter Cheney, "Canadian Fails Attempting Record Dive of 91 Meters in One Breath," *Globe and Mail*, April 28, 2008, A7.
5. Sam Kashner, "Her Monsters," *Vanity Fair*, November 2010, 172.
6. Christopher K. Germer, *The Mindful Path to Self-Compassion* (New York: Guilford, 2009), 2.

Chapter Three

1. Russell Lewis, *Margaret Thatcher: A Personal and Political Biography* (London: Routledge & Kegan Paul PLC, 1975), 11.
2. Heather Howell and Kim Stephens, *Your Journey to Executive: Insights from IBM Women Executives from the 2012–2013 Advancing Women at IBM Executive Research Study*, IBM, August 2013, 3, www03.ibm.com/employment/us/diverse/downloads/advancing_women_at_IBM_study_external_final.pdf.

3. From a conversation with Craig Barrett, then CEO of Intel, at an International Women's Forum conference in Las Vegas, 2004.

4. Jacquie McNish, "How a Spunky Newfoundlander Seized the 'Opportunity of a Life Time' at Britain's Royal Mail," *Globe and Mail*, October 13, 2010.

Chapter Four

1. Jacob Weisberg, "Yahoo's Marissa Mayer: Hail to the Chief," *Vogue*, September 2013, 824–25.

2. Rosener, "Ways Women Lead," 5.

3. Susan Dominus, "Exile on Park Avenue: How the JPMorgan Chase Trading Fiasco Took Down the Most Powerful Woman on Wall Street," *New York Times Magazine*, October 7, 2012, 36.

4. George Anders, "The Reluctant Savior of Hewlett-Packard," *Forbes*, June 10, 2013, 66.

Chapter Five

1. Adam Belz, "Facebook's Sandberg Calls on Women to Be Aggressive Leaders," *Star Tribune*, October 3, 2013. The article references Sandberg's speech at the Grace Hopper Celebration of Women in Computing in Minneapolis, Minnesota.

2. Kelly Wallace, "More People Prefer a Male Boss, but Gender Gap Is Narrowing," *CNN Living*, www.cnn.com/2013/11/13/living/identity-gallup-male-boss-female-boss/.

3. Huffington, *On Becoming Fearless*, 93.

4. Sheryl Sandberg, TEDWomen 2013, http://tedconfblog.files.wordpress.com/2013/12 /20131205_mca_9632.jpg.

5. Debra A. Benton, *Lions Don't Need to Roar* (New York: Warner Books, 1992).

Chapter Six

1. Nancy M. Carter and Christine Silva, "The Myth of the Ideal Worker: Does Doing All the Right Things Really Get Women Ahead?" *Catalyst*, 2011, 8.

2. Korkki, "For Women, Parity Is Still a Subtly Steep Climb."

3. Peggy Klaus, *Brag! The Art of Tooting Your Own Horn without Blowing It* (New York: Warner Business Books, 2003), xviii.

4. Nina Munk, "Why Women Find Lauder Mesmerizing," *Fortune*, May 25, 1998, 97.

5. Ibid.

Chapter Seven

1. Laurence Arnold, "Karen Strauss Cook, Goldman Trader Who Backed Moms, Dies at 61," www.bloomberg.com/news/2013–10–07/Karen-strauss-cook-goldman-who -backed-moms.

2. Bryant, "Corner Office," 6.

Chapter Eight

1. Candace West, "Against Our Will: Male Interruptions of Females in Cross-Sex Conversations," *Annals of the New York Academy of Sciences* 327 (June 1979), 81–96. These results were recorded in a laboratory setting. In a previous study by the author in "natural settings," men interrupted women in a full 96 percent of the cases. Similar conclusions are drawn by Kristin J. Anderson and Campbell Leaper in their study, "Meta-Analyses of Gender Effects on Conversational Interruption: Who, When, Where, and How," *Sex Roles: A Journal of Research* 39, nos. 3–4 (1998). Abstract of West's paper available at http://link.springer.com/article/10.1023/A:1018802521676#.

2. Barbara Annis and John Gray, *Work with Me: The 8 Blind Spots between Men and Women in Business* (New York: Palgrave Macmillan, 2013), 138–39.

3. Ibid., 139.

4. Kenneth Harris, *Thatcher* (London: Weidenfeld & Nicolson, 1988), 83.

5. Ibid., 83–84.

6. John Heilpern, "It's the Money Honey," *Vanity Fair*, September 2010, 144; and Chris Ariens, "Maria Bartiromo Abandoning 'Money Honey' Trademark?" *TV Newser*, March 28, 2010, www.mediabistro.com/tvnewser/maria-bartiromo-abandoning-money -honey-trademark_b25015.

Chapter Nine

1. Laura Sabattini, "Unwritten Rules: What You Don't Know Can Hurt Your Career," *Catalyst*, 2008, 5.

2. Joshua Green, "Joshua Green on Politics," *Bloomberg Business Week*, www .businessweek.com/articles/2013–02–25.

3. Eve MacSweeney, "Show and Tell," *Vogue*, August 2011, 156.

4. Bethany McLean, "Yahoo's Geek Goddess," *Vanity Fair*, January 2014, 70, www .vanityfair.com/business/2014/01/marissa-mayer-yahoo-google.

5. Dilma Rousseff at the UN General Assembly, September 21, 2011, www .teachthatspeech.com/.

6. Ginni Rometty, IBM's Chairman, President and Chief Executive Officer, 2013 Annual Meeting of Stockholders, www.ibm.com/ibm/ginni/04_30_2013.html.

7. Alexei Oreskovic and Peter Lauria, "Yahoo Turns to Google's Mayer for Revival," *Reuters*, www.reuters.com/article/2012/07/17/us-yahoo-ceo-idUSBRE86F13T20120717.

Chapter Ten

1. Margaret Thatcher, "Margaret Thatcher—Voice Before-and-After Lessons," BBC videoclip, www.youtube.com/watch?v=28_0gXLKLbk.

2. Annis and Gray, *Work with Me*, 114.

3. James W. Pennebaker, "Your Use of Pronouns Reveals Your Personality," *Harvard Business Review*, December 2011, 33.
4. Ibid., 32.
5. Leah Eichler, "'We' versus 'I': The Language of Leadership," *Globe and Mail*, Report on Business, July 14, 2012, B15.

Chapter Eleven

1. See www.thehumphreygroup.com.

Chapter Fourteen

1. Sabattini, "Unwritten Rules."

Chapter Sixteen

1. Margaret Thatcher, *The Path to Power* (London: HarperCollins Publishers, 1995), 295.
2. Ibid.
3. www.youtube.com/watch?v=aFxKt1sexVc.

Chapter Nineteen

1. Jessica Grose, "She Turned Her Upspeak Down a Notch," *New York Times*, July 28, 2013, 7.
2. A. M. Sperber and Eric Lax, "Bogart & Bacall," excerpt from their book, *Bogart*, in *Vanity Fair*, February 1997; www.vanityfair.com/hollywood/features/1997/02/bogart -bacall-excerpt-199702.
3. Blake Green, "That Classic Voice, That Timeless Look," *Toronto Star*, December 19, 1999, D10.
4. Max Atkinson, *Our Masters' Voices: The Language and Body Language of Politics* (London: Routledge, 1984). See chapter, "Margaret Thatcher and the Evolution of Charismatic Woman." Also see Max Atkinson's blog, "Margaret Thatcher and the Evolution of Charismatic Woman," http://maxatkinson.blogspot.ca/2009/01/margaret -thatcher-and-creation-of.html.
5. Atkinson blog, "Margaret Thatcher and the Evolution of Charismatic Woman."

Chapter Twenty

1. *My Fair Lady* is a musical based on George Bernard Shaw's *Pygmalion*, with book and lyrics by Alan Jay Lerner and music by Frederick Loewe.
2. **Articulate** (v) meaning "to divide speech into distinct parts" dates back to the 1590s from Latin *articulatus*, past participle of *articulare* "to separate into joints"; also "to utter distinctly," from *articulus* "joint."
3. W. S. Gilbert and Arthur Sullivan, *The Mikado*, Act I, "I Am So Proud," 1885.

Chapter Twenty-One

1. Sheryl Sandberg with Nell Scovell, *Lean In* (New York: Knopf, 2013).
2. Sheryl Sandberg, "Why We Have Too Few Women Leaders," TEDWomen 2010; "So We Leaned In . . . Now What?" TEDWomen 2013.
3. Malala Yousafzai. See her speech to the United Nations, July 12, 2013, www.youtube .com/watch?v=QRh_30C8l6Y.
4. Simone De Beauvoir, *The Second Sex* (New York: Vintage Books, 1989).

Chapter Twenty-Two

1. Kay and Shipman, *The Confidence Code*, 19.
2. TED.com. See also tedwomen.com for speeches that show how women and girls are reshaping the future.
3. See Maria Gonzalez, *Mindful Leadership* (Toronto: John Wiley and Sons, 2012).
4. Meryl Streep, Convocation Address at Indiana University, April 16, 2014, http:// www.theguardian.com/film/2014/apr/23/meryl-streep-i-thought-i-was-too-ugly-to-be -an-actress.
5. Susan Cain, "'An Introvert Steps Out': How the Author of 'Quiet' Delivered a Rousing Speech," *New York Times*, April 27, 2012.
6. Susan Cain, "The Power of Introverts," TED, February 2012, www.ted.com/talks /susan_cain_the_power_of_introverts.
7. David Mamet, *True and False: Heresy and Common Sense for the Actor* (New York: Vintage Books, 1997), 59.

Chapter Twenty-Three

1. There are many articles and books that show a correlation between business success and physical height. See Arianne Cohen, *The Tall Book* (New York: Bloomsbury, 2009); Del Jones, "Does Height Equal Power? Some CEOs Say Yes," *USA Today*, July 17, 2007, http://usatoday30.usatoday.com/money/companies/management /2007–07–17-ceo-dominant-behavior_N.htm; Jenna Goudreau, "The Seven Ways Your Boss Is Judging Your Appearance," *Forbes*, November 30, 2012, www.forbes.com /sites/jennagoudreau/2012/11/30/the-seven-ways-your-boss-is-judging-your-appearance.
2. Melinda French Gates, "What Non-Profits Can Learn from Coca Cola," www.TEDx .com, uploaded October 12, 2010; www.youtube.com/watch?v=GlUS6KE67Vs.

Chapter Twenty-Four

1. See http://center-for-nonverbal-studies.org/headside.htm.
2. Susan Shellenbarger, "Is the Boss Looking at You? You'd Better Hope So," *Wall Street Journal*, posted May 29, 2013, at http://blogs.wsj.com/atwork/2013/05/29/is-the-boss

-looking-at-you-youd-better-hope-so/. The article points to several studies that show a strong correlation between status and eye contact.

3. Susan Shellenbarger, "Why Eye Contact Matters," *Wall Street Journal*, reprinted in the *Globe and Mail*, May 31, 2013, B12.

4. Misty Harris, "Why a Big Grin May Not Be So Great," *Edmonton Journal*, August 20, 2012.

Chapter Twenty-Five

1. Shereen Dindar, "Law Firm's Memo to Female Employees Blasted as Sexist," *Shine On*; http://ca.shine.yahoo.com/blogs/shine-on/law-firm-memo-female-employees-blasted -sexist-163345346.html.

2. Katya Wachtel, "That Crazy 44-Page Long UBS Dress Code Got Ridiculed So Much That Now It's Getting 'Revised,'" *Business Insider*, January 18, 2011, www .businessinsider.com/swiss-bank-ubs-changes-much-mocked-dress-code-garlic -underwear-smell-shower-january-2011-1.

3. Elizabeth Dwoskin, "Is This Woman Too Hot to Be a Banker?" *Village Voice*, June 1, 2010, www.villagevoice/cp,/2010–06–01/news/is-this-woman-too-hot . . .

4. Irving Dejohn, Kerry Burke, and Corky Siemaszko, "Too Sexy for New York? Woman Says She Was Fired for Being Too Busty," *New York Daily News*, May 21, 2012, www .nydailynews.com/new-york/sexy-new-york-woman-fired-busty-article-1.1082045.

5. Annis and Gray, *Work with Me*, 71.

Conclusion

1. William Shakespeare, *As You Like It*, Act II, scene vii, 139–40. Quoted in John Bartlett, *Familiar Quotations*, 16th ed. (Boston: Little, Brown, 1992), 191.

2. Rosabeth Moss Kanter, *Evolve! Succeeding in the Digital Culture of Tomorrow* (Boston: Harvard University Press, 2001), 111.

3. Mamet, *True and False*, 39.

4. http://lens.blogs.nytimes.com/2013/05/09/across-the-border-live-and-in-color/.

5. Mamet, *True and False*, 47.

Acknowledgments

T his book is a collaboration of many "voices," and its rich texture reflects the breadth of these contributions.

The Humphrey Group team has provided amazing guidance to me every step of the way. I particularly thank Nicky Guadagni and Maggie Huculak, seasoned instructors who generously contributed anecdotes and insights from their classroom experience. They also read the chapters and provided illuminating content for the book. Others in the company who contributed thoughtful insights to the book are Brenda Allen, Vanessa AvRuskin, Linda Griffiths, Elissa Lansdell, Kate Lynch, and Jocelyn Zucco—all of whom teach Taking the Stage®. Their passion for this program, their work with clients, and their deep knowledge of theater techniques—particularly in areas such as voice and presence—helped shape the book. I also thank Dan Dumsha for providing insights for chapter 23.

I'm grateful as well to the many corporations that have sponsored our Taking the Stage programs throughout the world—and who have provided valuable feedback. These include Bank of America, Best Buy, CEVA Logistics, CIBC, Corning, Dell, GDF Suez, Goldcorp, HSBC, IBM, Ontario Power Generation, Wal-Mart Mexico, TD, and RBC. I also extend my appreciation to IBM, for partnering with The Humphrey Group to develop a format that allows delivery of our women's programs with in-house facilitators. Melissa Downer, IBM software director, speaks for many of these "mentors" when she says, "I have had the opportunity to be a coleader of Taking the Stage and found it to be a great way to bring a strong group of females together for some valuable professional development. As women, we need to have the confidence to stand up and have a voice equal to that of our male counterparts."

I thank the women around the world who have generously shared their stories with me. The examples of courage, boldness, assertiveness, and success that provide the rich texture of this book come from women in every geographical region of the world and at all levels of corporate life and beyond. Indeed, because they shared their stories, readers can see that taking the stage has positive, real-life outcomes.

I owe much, as well, to my private coaching clients who over the years have provided a lens through which I have come to understand how women communicate. This has been very special and privileged work, and many of the insights in this book come from these senior women who have shared their thoughts and aspirational goals with me.

Although much of this book reflects our work with women, I've also reached out to senior men and asked for their comments on the challenges and opportunities that affect the lives of corporate women. These male leaders, all of whom support the advancement of women in their organizations, generously shared their experiences. In particular, I am grateful to Steve Dyer, CFO of Agrium, Inc.; Tom Marinelli, acting CEO and chief transformation officer of Ontario Lottery and Gaming Corporation; John Montalbano, CEO of RBC Global Asset Management; Richard Nesbitt, CEO of CIBC World Markets; and Jay Redman, principal of PRISM Consulting. They are quoted in the text and their insights are reflected in the "Advice for Leaders of Women" sections.

I'm also indebted to those individuals who painstakingly read drafts of the book and offered valuable advice. Several of my colleagues at The Humphrey Group—Brenda Allen, Cynthia Ward, Niamh Farrelly, and Fang Yu—scrutinized much of the manuscript, as did Liz Reynolds, diversity manager at KPMG (Toronto). These women helped out even before I promised them a "day at the spa." I also want to thank Cathryn Gabor, a principal at Korn Ferry (Houston), who led many Taking the Stage sessions, read my manuscript, and provided excellent case studies for the book.

My husband, Marc Egnal, read, reread, and provided editorial guidance for every chapter—even when I didn't want more suggestions! He stood by me as I devoted an intensive year to writing this book— much of it holed up in our Mexican home. Our sons, Bart Egnal and

Ben Egnal, were a source of strength and pride: Bart as the new CEO of The Humphrey Group gave me the time and resources I needed to write this book, and the satisfaction of knowing he is leading the company to new heights. Ben as a young advertising talent allowed me to feel a shared sense of creativity as he pursues his own "big ideas." Higgins, our pug, slept happily through it all, curled up at my feet.

The team at Wiley/Jossey-Bass provided superb support. Senior editor Karen Murphy assembled an extraordinarily skilled and supportive team. Christine Moore, my developmental editor, always responded enthusiastically, quickly, and with editorial insight to virtually every line of the manuscript. She even did the exercises in the book! Assistant editor John Maas was everything a writer can wish for: enthusiastic, positive, warm, generous with his ideas and in accepting mine. Mark Karmendy, production manager, organized my life through the entire production process and graciously tolerated my revisions, as did Pam Suwinsky, my copyeditor, who went through the book with a fine-tooth comb. It has been an exciting collaborative process, and I feel fortunate to have a team of such seasoned and talented professionals, and to be working again with John Wiley and Sons, who also published my first book.

It's an honor to share the stage with such an amazing "cast of characters" and to know readers will benefit from the collective wisdom that has shaped this book. My thanks to everyone who has been involved in this grand production.

About the Author

J udith Humphrey is founder and chief creative officer of The Humphrey Group Inc., a firm that for twenty-five years has taught executives and leaders to influence and inspire their audiences.

The Humphrey Group grew out of Judith's vision that communications needed to be taught from a leadership *perspective*—ensuring that every act of speaking is an act of leadership. The Humphrey Group brings together the two areas and shows clients how to express their leadership through strong communications. The company's trademarked programs include Speaking as a Leader; Communication for the Senior Leader; Leadership Conversations; and Leadership Presence. The Humphrey Group also partners with The Niagara Institute to deliver its programs.

Taking the Stage and Succeeding on Stage, the firm's pioneering programs for women, have reached half a million women around the world in the past decade. These women have discovered their own power and confidence as a result of learning to speak up, stand out, and advance their careers. Judith has a deep personal connection to these women's programs because she, too, has taken the stage throughout her life—as a violinist, university lecturer, and head of a communications firm.

Judith has an MA in English literature from The University of Rochester. Her work has been reprinted in *Vital Speeches,* and she is the author of *Speaking as a Leader: How to Lead Every Time You Speak* (Jossey-Bass, 2012). In 2012 the YWCA of Toronto honored her as "Entrepreneur of the Year." Judith lives with her husband, Marc, in

Toronto and Mexico; they have two sons, Bart and Ben Egnal, and an extended and cherished family that includes Emily Mather, Fang Yu, grandson Kye Egnal, and a black pug, Higgins.

The Humphrey Group has offices in Toronto, Vancouver, Calgary, and Mexico City. For more information on the firm, see www.thehum phreygroup.com.

Index

A

Addiction to Perfection (Woodman), 20

Advice for leaders of women: dealing with women's inner crow, 26–27; encouraging appropriate body language, 189; encouraging articulation, 158; encouraging awareness of language, 94–95; encouraging career conversations, 115–116; encouraging courage, 64–65; encouraging vocal power, 135–136; encouraging women to be assertive, 46–47; encouraging women to develop a strong stance, 182; encouraging women to have a strong script, 101; encouraging women to hold their ground, 74–75; encouraging women to move to center stage, 33; encouraging women to portray themselves as leaders, 86–87; encouraging women to speak up, 41; encouraging women to stand out, 18–19; encouraging women's expressiveness, 154; encouraging women's voices, 129, 142, 147; helping women express themselves in meetings, 107–108; helping women gain a strong presence, 165–166; helping women with stage fright, 173–174; mentoring a dress style, 196–197; mentoring women in elevator scripts, 122; mentoring women in self-promotion, 58

Aggressiveness: vs. assertiveness, 42–43; avoiding, 44–46

Ambition, 31

Ambivalence, 55

Annis, Barbara, 67, 197

Apologizing, 89, 93

Articulation, 155–158

Asking questions, 89–90, 93